Schrader-Motor-Chronik

CHEVROLET CORVETTE

1953–86

143
216 VW 75

Schrader-Motor-Chronik

CHEVROLET CORVETTE
1953–86

Dokumentation: Walter Zeichner

Schrader Verlag

Als den einzig echten Sportwagen Amerikas apostrophierte General Motors den rassigen Zweisitzer bei seiner Vorstellung im Jahre 1953. In der Tat gehörte dieser Wagen zum Faszinierendsten, was Detroit je zu bieten hatte. Ein Querschnitt durch die Fülle der mit Liebe ausgewählten und in diesem Buch wiedergegebenen Werbemittel und Presseberichte dreier Jahrzehnte macht deutlich, warum die Corvette so erfolgreich war. Denn dieses Auto war alles andere als der ,,typische Amischlitten'' – die Corvette galt stets als ein Fahrzeug mit eigenem Charakter.

Die Zusammenstellung der Dokumente besorgte Walter Zeichner mit Unterstützung durch Kai Jacobsen, dem hierfür besonderer Dank ausgesprochen sei.

Halwart Schrader
Herausgeber

Neudruck der 1989 im Verlag Schrader Automobil-Bücher Handels GmbH, München, erschienenen Originalausgabe

Dokumentation: Walter Zeichner
Satz und Druck: Bosch-Druck, Landshut/Ergolding
ISBN 3-922617-51-4
Printed in Germany

Inhalt

Ein Sportwagen made in U.S.A.

Die Corvette war und ist auch heute der einzige echte Sportwagen aus amerikanischer Produktion, sieht man einmal von ein paar kurzlebigen ,,Eintagsfliegen'' ab. Es erstaunt diese Tatsache um so mehr, denkt man an den hohen Stellenwert, den der Motorsport in den USA seit jeher einnimmt.
Dabei bestand zwar schon immer ein sehr hoher Bedarf an Sportwagen, der aber fast ausschließlich durch Fabrikate europäischer Herkunft gedeckt wurde.
Die Entstehungsgeschichte der Chevrolet Corvette ist eng verknüpft mit dem Designer Harley Earl, der schon 1951 die Idee zu einem preiswerten, einfach herzustellenden Sportwagen gehabt hatte und der es schließlich durchsetzen konnte, daß solch ein Wagen auch tatsächlich gebaut wurde.
Earl war 1932, nach dem Studium in Stanford und einer Zeit, in der er Spezialkarosserien für eine extravagante Clientel in Hollywood gezeichnet hatte, zu General Motors gestoßen. Er hatte dort ein Design Center aufgebaut, das damals seinesgleichen suchte und in dem Leute arbeiteten, die den Stil der amerikanischen Automobile maßgebend beeinflußten; Maßstäbe setzten dabei die anläßlich von Shows und Motoramas gezeigten ,,Dream Cars'', Wagen mit auffällig futuristischem Styling und verspielten Details, die einen Blick in die Zukunft des Automobils, jedenfalls in den USA, gewähren ließen und um die sich ein autobegeistertes Publikum drängte. Solche Schöpfungen waren eine Spezialität Harvey Earls. Mit seinem 1938 vorgestellten ,,Buick Y-Job'' beeinflußte er das Ideal amerikanischer Autobaukunst bis in die späten vierziger Jahre.
Nach dem zweiten Weltkrieg, nachdem die amerikanischen Automobilgiganten voll mit der Produktion von Kriegsmaterial beschäftigt gewesen waren und die Herstellung von Zivilfahrzeugen geruht hatte, wurde erst einmal mit den alten Modellen die Produktion fortgesetzt, bevor mit Beginn der fünfziger Jahre bei allen amerikanischen Automobil-Herstellern neue Stilelemente sichtbar wurden.
Einer dieser Trendsetter war der von Earl entworfene Buick ,,Le Sabre'', ein vom Düsenjäger-Styling beeinflußter Prototyp, der 1951 auf den Shows für Furore sorgte und von dem sich einige markante Merkmale, wie die extremen Panoramascheiben und das unter einem Deckel verschwindende Faltdach, auf die spätere Corvette vererben sollten.
Im gleichen Jahr hatte Harvey Earl mit einem kleinen Stab persönlicher Mitarbeiter in einem separaten Studio mit der Entwicklung seines Sportwagens begonnen. Zuerst war geplant, einen Zweisitzer zu bauen, der in der Preislage normaler Chevrolet- oder Ford-Limousinen rangierte. Erste Zeichnungen zeigten ein Auto, das wie eine Kreuzung zwischen Jaguar XK 120 und Jeepster aussah und auf einem normalen Chassis der laufenden Limousinenreihe basierte. Die Arbeiten liefen unter der Bezeichnung ,,Projekt Opel'', denn man legte auf strenge Geheimhaltung auch innerhalb des Konzerns Wert, der für die deutsche Tochter schon öfter Design-Arbeiten übernommen hatte.
1952 stieß mit Edward Cole ein Konstrukteur zum Team, der die technische Seite der künftigen Corvette prägen sollte; bald arbeiteten beide Abteilungen eng zusammen. Earls Mannschaft kam immer weiter von der ersten nüchternen Planung ab und orientierte sich stilmäßig nun stark an Dream Cars wie Buick Le Sabre und dem neuen Typ XP-300, einem noch futuristischeren Modell.
Es wurde indessen vorausgesetzt, daß der Wagen mit dem geringsten Aufwand an neu zu konstruierenden Teilen herzustellen war, denn in den Chefetagen wäre ein kostspieliges ,,Spielzeug'', von dem keine sehr hohen Stückzahlen zu erwarten waren, sonst auf taube Ohren gestoßen. So mußte in dem Sinne konstruiert werden, daß möglichst viele Teile ,,aus dem Regal'' der aktuellen

Da freut sich die Frau Gemahlin des Generaldirektors – so ungefähr konnte die Bildaussage dieses Pressefotos aus dem Jahre 1960 lauten. Zentralverschluß-Attrappen und Weißwandreifen waren stets beliebt.

Produktionsteile zu nehmen waren, was so gut wie alle mechanischen Teile und das Chassis betraf. Auch die Karosserie sollte so preisgünstig wie möglich zu bauen sein.

Nun hatte man bei der Chevrolet Division gerade ein großes Cabriolet mit verstärkter Fiberglas-Karosserie ge-

Das 1964er Sting Ray Coupé. War Fliegen schöner? Der Flugkapitän und die Stewardeß hätten zugunsten der Corvette gestimmt . . .

testet. Das neue Material hatte sogar einen unfreiwilligen Überschlag des Testfahrers fast unbeschädigt überstanden. Harley Earl kam dies wie gerufen, denn durch dieses leicht zu formende, neue Material waren enorme Kosten für Karosseriewerkzeuge einzusparen, womit sein ,,Baby'' ein noch geringeres Investitionsrisiko für das Unternehmen darstellen würde. Die Chancen für grünes Licht zur Serienproduktion stiegen; wie sich das Kunststoffmaterial dann im jahrelangen Alltagsbetrieb benehmen würde, war eine andere Frage.

Inzwischen war es Sommer 1952 geworden, und ein fertiges Tonmodell des neuen Zweisitzers stand in der Entwicklungsabteilung des Art & Color Studios. Auch Chevrolet-Chefingenieur Ed Cole war begeistert von dem Wagen. Nun kam der große Moment – die Präsentation des Wagens vor General-Motors-Präsident Harlow Curtice und der Chevrolet-Vorstandschaft. Der neue Sportwagen gefiel den hohen Herren so gut, daß ein Prototyp in Auftrag gegeben wurde, um ihn anläßlich des ersten Motoramas der Öffentlichkeit zu präsentieren. Man versprach sich durch solch einen Wagen vor allem auch eine Imageverbesserung der ganzen Chevrolet-Linie.

Auf Hochtouren wurde jetzt an der Fertigstellung des Prototyps gearbeitet, der ja auch unter der Haube voll funktionsfähig sein mußte. Fahrwerkspezialist Maurice Olley schaffte es, ein passendes Chassis und eine Radaufhängung weitgehend aus Serienteilen zu bauen, die

nur leicht für die Anforderungen eines Sportwagens modifiziert waren. Das wirkte sich positiv auf die Kosten aus, wenngleich der Wagen in konstruktiver Hinsicht mit den europäischen Produkten nicht mithalten konnte.
Am 17. Januar 1953 wurde schließlich der Schleier gelüftet. Im großen Ballsaal des New Yorker Waldorf-Astoria-Hotels drängten sich die Besucher der ersten Motorama des Jahres vor dem weißen Roadster von Chevrolet. Der Radstand des „Corvette" genannten Zweisitzers entsprach genau dem des Jaguar XK 120, doch war der Wagen breiter und wuchtiger. Man hatte es deutlich vermieden, Stylinganleihen aus dem europäischen Sportwagenbau zu übernehmen, und ein typisch amerikanisches Auto geschaffen. Um die Gewichtsverteilung zu optimieren, lagen die Sitze direkt vor der Hinterachse. Der Motor, ein frisierter „Blue Flame" Sechszylinder mit 150 PS Leistung, konnte weit hinten installiert werden, so daß sich das Gewicht 53 zu 47 auf Vorder- und Hinterachse verteilen ließ. Ein Kühlermaul mit großen Chromzähnen beherrschte die Front, die nur von Stoßstangenhörnern rechts und links des Nummernschildes und an den Ecken geschützt wurde; sportliche Steinschlaggitter zierten die ovalen, tief in die runden Vorderkotflügel integrierten Scheinwerfer.
Eine niedrige Panoramascheibe begrenzte den mit rotem Kunstleder ausgeschlagenen Innenraum, deren Chromrahmen sich in einen das ganze Cockpit umfassenden Ring fortsetzte. Auch das Armaturenbrett erinnerte sehr an Dream Cars. Links war der Tacho eingebaut, während rechts Lautsprecher und Ablagefach untergebracht waren. Dazwischen schauten den Passagieren nicht weniger als sechs Anzeigeinstrumente entgegen, das größte davon in der Mitte war der Drehzahlmesser. Die Schalensitze waren eingebettet in die Karosserie, und die Türen des Prototyps öffneten sich auf Knopfdruck. Das leichte Verdeck mit Steckscheiben verschwand unter einem Deckel hinter den Sitzen. Das Heck lief rund aus wie die Front, nur waren hier deutliche Flossen einmodelliert worden mit runden Heckleuchten an der Spitze und kleinen Torpedoflügeln. Die großen Radausschnitte gaben freien Blick auf die Weißwandreifen, und eine von den vorderen zu den hinteren Stoßfängern laufende seitliche Zierleiste flankierte die großen Seitenflächen.
Es war ohne Zweifel ein sehr gelungenes und gefälliges Auto, das die Leute in New York bestaunen konnten. Fast vier Millionen begutachteten den neuen Typ. Die Reaktionen waren überwältigend. Harley Earl hatte seinen Traum verwirklicht – die Firmenleitung gab die Anweisung, die Corvette so schnell wie möglich in Produktion gehen zu lassen.
Noch im selben Jahr 1953 entstanden die ersten 300 Vorserienexemplare weitgehend in Handarbeit, während man in St. Louis eine neue Produktionsstraße einrichtete, die dann bis 1981 Geburtsort der Corvette bleiben sollte. Damals wurden die 46 Karosserieteile aus Glasfiber von einer Fremdfirma in Ohio gefertigt und dann von Hand zusammengeleimt, während die Motoren aus dem Chevrolet-Motorenwerk in New York stammten. Auch den Rahmenbau nahm eine Vertragsfirma vor. Diese ersten Wagen waren noch nicht perfekt in der Verarbeitung, und die ersten 25 hatten auch die Serienradkappen der Chevrolet „Bel Air" Limousine, bevor es eigene Radkappen für die Corvette mit Zentralverschluß-Attrappe gab (was viele indessen als wenig geschmackvoll empfanden). Alle 300 Wagen waren in Polo-Weiß gespritzt und hatten rot/weißes Interieur mit schwarzem Verdeck sowie Weißwandreifen.
Leider enttäuschte jedoch schon die ersten Tester und Eigentümer die Leistung des Wagens, der die hochgeschraubten Erwartungen keinesfalls zu erfüllen vermochte. Der Sechszylindermotor ließ den Wagen, der aus Kosten- und Platzgründen mit der bekannten Powerglide-Zweigangautomatik ausgerüstet war, nur

knapp 170 km/h erreichen. Auch eine Beschleunigungszeit von bestenfalls 11 Sekunden von 0 auf 100 km/h war nicht dazu geeignet, das verwöhnte amerikanische Publikum zu begeistern. Zugleich hatte man den geplant niedrigen Preis bei weitem nicht realisieren können, und so kostete der Roadster jetzt beachtliche 3513 Dollar.
Für das Modelljahr 1954 erfolgte dann die Produktion in St. Louis mit etwa 50 Wagen täglich. Im Laufe des Jahres erfuhr die Corvette dann schon einige Verbesserungen. Außer in Polo White konnte man den Sportwagen in Metallic-Blau haben, aber nur vier Prozent entschlossen sich für die dritte Möglichkeit, „Sportsman Red". Außerdem hatten von den 3640 Corvetten, die in diesem Jahr entstanden, nur sechs eine schwarze Sonderlackierung in Verbindung mit roter Innenausstattung.
Um die Türen der Serien-Corvette zu öffnen, gab es keinen Druckknopf mehr wie beim Prototyp, sondern man mußte – was vor allem bei geschlossenem Verdeck keine Freude bereitete – durchs Fenster greifen und den Innenhebel nach hinten ziehen. Verbessert wurde hingegen die Position des Choke, der bei den ersten Wagen noch rechts neben dem Anlaß-Schloß lag, so daß man mit der linken Hand durchs Lenkrad fassen mußte und gleichzeitig mit der rechten Hand den Zündschlüssel umdrehte. Das Verdeck präsentierte sich bei den 1954er Modellen braun.
Die Karosserie machte noch einige Sorgen, da es an manchen Stellen Wassereinbrüche zu verzeichnen gab, ein Mangel, der erst im Laufe dieses Modelljahres behoben werden konnte. Dennoch gab das Desinteresse des Publikums an der Corvette zu Sorgen Anlaß: Die Kritiker waren offenbar zu hart mit dem Auto umgegangen. Mittlerweile an europäische Formen und Hochleistungsmotoren gewöhnt, ließ man kaum ein gutes Haar am Chevrolet. Für einen Sportwagen fehlte dem Auto nach Meinung vieler die Rasanz. Die Automatik und der biedere Motor machten zusammen mit der bauchigen Karosserie einem Jaguar keine Konkurrenz, und auf der anderen Seite war das Auto zu unkomfortabel für einen Tourer. Ende 1954 standen immer noch fast 1500 Wagen bei den Händlern auf dem Hof. Doch für das Modelljahr 1955 gab es gute Nachrichten, denn auf Wunsch wurde nun der neue, von Ed Cole konstruierte V8-Motor eingebaut, der 195 PS brachte und dabei noch 15 Kilo leichter war als der alte Sechszylinder. Diese erste V8 Corvette brauchte nur noch 8,5 Sekunden für den Spurt auf 100 km/h – über mangelnde Power konnte man sich also nicht mehr beschweren.
Das Automatik-Getriebe entsprach dem Image eines Sportwagens ebenfalls nicht, doch es blieb zunächst im Programm. In diesem Modelljahr fanden sich nur 700 Käufer, von denen ganze zehn sich noch für den Sechszylinder entschieden. Wer einen „richtigen" Sportwagen wollte, hatte schließlich eine große Auswahl an schicken Wagen aus Europa, und wer es amerikanisch-gemütlich, aber trotzdem mit sportlicher Aufmachung und guter Leistung liebte, der kaufte sich den neuen Ford Thunderbird, der limousinenhafte Bequemlichkeit mit preudo-sportlichen Attributen perfekt kombinierte und sich mehr als 20mal so gut verkaufen ließ wie die Corvette, deren Tage schon gezählt schienen.
Doch General Motors wollte das Rennen gegen die Ford Company unter keinen Umständen verlieren. Schließlich trat ein Mann auf den Plan, der für viele Jahre die Geschicke dieses amerikanischen Sportwagens lenken sollte: Zora Arkus-Duntov. Der in Belgien geborene ehemalige Konstrukteur bei der englischen Sportwagenfirma Allard war im Geburtsjahr der Corvette zu GM gestoßen und hatte sich bald des erfolglosen Roadsters angenommen. Das neue Modell 1956 sollte er bereits entscheidend prägen. Vor allem wurde die Karosserie komplett überarbeitet, wobei die vordere Hälfte erhebliche Veränderungen erfuhr. Eine breite Mulde war in die Flanken einmodelliert worden, die vom Radausschnitt

bis fast unter die neuen Türgriffe reichte und in kontrastierender Farbe gespritzt wurde. Die Scheinwerfer standen jetzt senkrecht und hatten keine Schutzgitter mehr. Am Heck waren die Flossen weggefallen, und übrig blieben schön geschwungene Kotflügel, an deren Enden die beiden Auspuffrohre mündeten, die beim Vormodell neben dem Kofferdeckel ins Freie geragt hatten und durch Verwirbelungen der Abgase stets für ein verschmutztes Heck des Roadsters gesorgt hatten. Für die komfortbewußten amerikanischen Sportfahrer hatte der Wagen nun auch Kurbelfenster, und auf Wunsch machte ein Hardtop die Corvette zum Coupé.

Der Wagen konnte jetzt in sieben Farben bestellt werden mit mehr oder weniger geschmackvollen Interieur-Varianten. Doch beschränkten sich die Veränderungen für die Corvette der zweiten Generation keineswegs auf Äußerlichkeiten. Der aktive Rennfahrer Arkus-Duntov hatte seine Aufmerksamkeit merklich den Fahreigenschaften gewidmet (nur die Bremsen waren leider immer noch weit überfordert und reagierten bei sportlicher Fahrweise schnell mit Fading). Vor allem aber hatte die Corvette jetzt eine Dreigang-Schaltung anstatt der Automatik bekommen, zusammen mit einem in der Leistung abermals angehobenen Motor. Der heißeste Limousinenmotor mit Vierfachvergaser war durch den Einbau einer von Duntov ,,verschärften" Nockenwelle auf 225 PS bei 5200/min getunt worden; mit dem Schaltgetriebe stürmte die neue Corvette nun in beachtlichen 7,5 Sekunden auf 100 km/h und dies sogar mit der langen Übersetzung von 3,27 : 1.

1958 gab es erneut ein deutliches Face-lifting mit Doppelscheinwerfern, zusätzlichen Lufteinlässen vorne und reichlich mehr Chromzierat; alles in allem wurde der Wagen dadurch fast einen Zentner schwerer, aber kaum schöner; er wirkte jetzt reichlich überladen. Innen gab es ein völlig neues Armaturenbrett in Form zweier halbrunder Einbuchtungen. Die rechte war mit einer dicken Haltestange versperrt, an der sich der Beifahrer bei kühnen Manövern festklammern konnte, und auf der Fahrerseite waren nun alle Anzeigeinstrumente außer der Uhr versammelt, überragt vom riesigen, halbrunden Tacho.

Als Motorisierung gab es bis 1961 nur noch das 283-c.i.-Aggregat mit Leistungen zwischen 230 (mit Vierfachvergaser) und 315 PS (mit Benzineinspritzung). Keine Corvette war jetzt länger als 8 Sekunden bis zur 100-km/h-Marke unterwegs.

1961 – schon unter der Regie des neuen Chefdesigners Bill Mitchell, der die futuristischen Dream Cars ,,Stingray" und ,,XP-700" entworfen hatte – wurde die runde Heckpartie durch ein ,,ducktail"-Heck ersetzt. Der Trend ging zu eckigeren Formen. Im folgenden Jahr wurden die Seitenflächen schlichter, außerdem gab es wieder einen größeren Achtzylinder mit nun 327 c.i. Mit Vergasern gaben diese Motoren zwischen 250 und 340 PS ab, und eine mit 11,25 : 1 enorm hoch verdichtete Version mit Benzineinspritzung produzierte sogar 360 PS. Ein solcher Wagen kostete schon knapp über 5000 Dollar.

Stilistisch stark an den ,,Stingray"-Prototyp angelehnt, erschien 1963 die vierte Generation der Corvette in Form von Roadster, Hardtop und einem neuen Coupé mit ungewöhnlich gestyltem, spitz zulaufendem Fließheck mit Doppelfenster und weit ins Dach hineinreichenden Türen – heute eine der gesuchtesten Corvette-Varianten. Bill Mitchell hatte den neuen Stil geprägt, mit Haifischnase und -maul und im Vergleich zum Vormodell kantigerer Linienführung. Doch auch unter der Kunststoffhaut hatte sich viel getan. Ein neuer Leiterrahmen machte es möglich, die Sitze noch tiefer und weiter hinten unterzubringen, um die Gewichtsverteilung zu optimieren. Der Radstand war verkürzt worden, und hinten hatte man die Räder nun endlich einzeln aufgehängt, was die Straßenlage des Autos sehr verbesserte.

Für das Modelljahr 1963 hatte man die Motoren vom Vorjahr übernommen, doch ab 1964 und bis zum Ende dieser Karosserievariante 1967 fand nochmals eine wahre Leistungsorgie statt. 1964 gab es sechs Leistungsversionen des 327-c.i.-Motors von 250 bis 375 PS, doch das war erst der harmlose Anfang. 1965 – im gleichen Jahr gab es erstmals auf Wunsch Scheibenbremsen an allen vier Rädern – kam ein neuer 396-c.i.-Motor mit 425 Vergaser-PS, der zusammen mit einem Sportfahrwerk und optischen Signalen wie dickem Buckel auf der Motorhaube und Sidepipes den Chevy Sportwagen in ein aufregendes Vehikel verwandelte.
Ab jenem Jahr gab es aus Kostengründen keine Einspritzmotoren mehr, doch die Corvette hatte sich mittlerweile zu einem Verkaufsrenner entwickelt. Fast 120 000 Wagen wurden allein von dieser Karosserieversion verkauft, davon etwas über 72 000 Roadster.
Schon 1963/64 hatte man mit den Arbeiten an einem Nachfolgemodell begonnen. Es handelte sich um ein wunderschönes Mittelmotor-Versuchsmodell mit der Bezeichnung „XP-882", das jedoch wenig später aus Kostengründen zu den Akten gelegt wurde. Die neue Corvette wurde weiterhin konventionell gebaut. Als Vorbild diente die schon fast bösartig aussehende Styling-Studie „Mako Shark II" von 1965, die unter der Regie des neuen Art-Directors David Holls zu einem etwas gemäßigteren, wenn auch immer noch äußerst aggressiv wirkenden Sportwagen geformt wurde.
Die Kritiker hatten stets viel zu bemängeln gehabt an der hierzulande vielleicht bekanntesten Corvette-Form. Sie war ihnen zu groß, zu altmodisch, und im Innenraum gab es zu wenig Platz für Passagiere und Gepäck. Trotzdem ließen sich im Modelljahr 1968 immerhin 28 566 Käufer nicht von einem Kauf abhalten – ein neuer Rekord. Bis 1983 wurde diese Karosserie mit zahlreichen Veränderungen gebaut. Es gab drei Varianten bis zum Wegfall des Roadsters 1976, nämlich zusätzlich ein „T-Top" Cabrio mit abnehmbaren Dachhälften sowie ein Coupé.
Scharfe Abgasgesetze drückten die Leistung der stärksten Version 1972 auf 365 PS, und nach einigen Zwischenstationen und auf Grund des Ölschocks war man 1975 bei 205 PS angelangt. Die Corvette war vom bärenstarken „muscle car" zu einem mit allen erdenklichen Extras ausrüstbaren Einkaufswagen sportlicher Hausfrauen geworden, wenn auch nur höchstens zwei volle Supermarkttüten unterzubringen waren. Kein Wunder, daß sich immer weniger Käufer für den übergewichtigen und im Vergleich zu früher lahmen Sportwagen interessierten. So sank die Verkaufszahl 1975 – es war das letzte Jahr des Stingray-Roadsters – auf magere 4629 Exemplare.
Es sollte nun fast zehn Jahre dauern, ehe eine völlig neue Corvette das Licht der Welt erblicken durfte, entwickelt von einem neuen Team von Konstrukteuren und Designern – unbelasted durch die Vergangenheit. Das betont niedrige und breite Coupé, das 1983 die sechste Generation dieses Sportwagens begründete, war wiederum von zahlreichen Show Cars inspiriert worden, und man muß zugeben, daß es ein sehr beeindruckender Wagen geworden ist. Er läßt die traditionellen Merkmale der Corvette, symbolisierte Kraft und sprungbereites Lauern, wieder aufleben. 1978 hatte man mit der intensiven Entwicklungsarbeit an diesem keilförmigen Wagen begonnen, der unter deutlichem Einfluß des Windkanals entstand. Er ist außer in der Breite in jeder Dimension kleiner als der Stingray, wirkt jedoch durch geschickte Verschiebung der Proportionen höchstens zierlicher. Endpunkt in der Styling-Entwicklung der neuen 230-PS-Corvette war schließlich 1986 die Präsentation der Roadster-Version, der ersten seit zehn Jahren. Es war dies ein modernes, gekonnt geformtes Fahrzeug – würdig, die Reihe beeindruckender offener Sportwagen von Chevrolet seit 1953 fortzusetzen.

Bescheidener Anfang

Mit dem herkömmlichen Sechszylinder-Chevi-Motor – wenn auch mit 150 PS – war die Corvette kein allzu heißes Eisen. Und trotz des enormen Interesses, das der Wagen anläßlich seiner Präsentation geweckt hatte, gab es 1953–54 nur knapp 4000 Käufer für dieses Auto. Aber auch die Produktionsmöglichkeiten waren anfangs begrenzt.

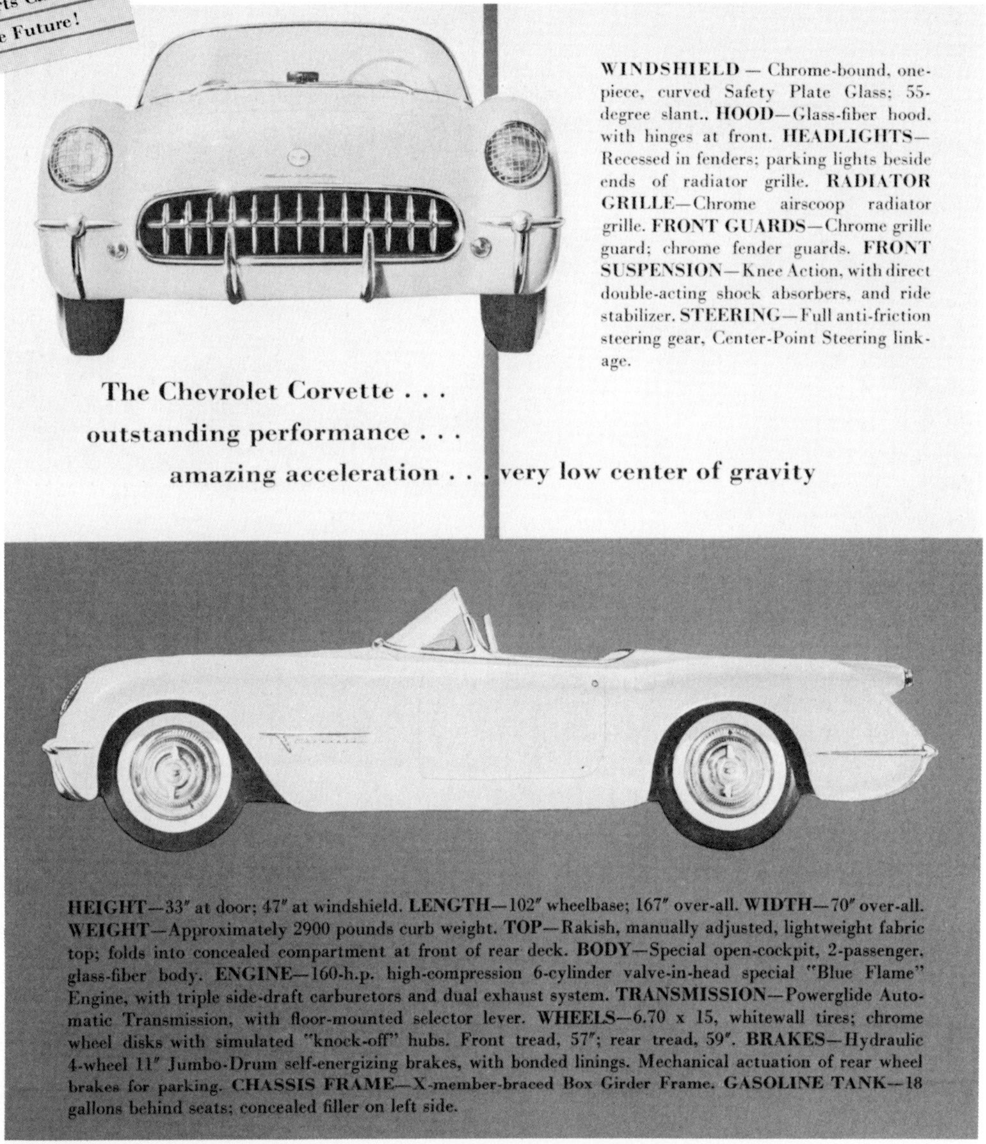

Wenig aufwendig gibt sich der erste Prospekt, der anläßlich der Produktionsaufnahme im Sommer 1953 von General Motors herausgegeben wurde. Stolz wird auf die vielen Chromteile verwiesen.

Real driving comfort . . . the Corvette way!

SECURITY AND LUXURY for driver and passenger are the keynotes of the snug Corvette cockpit. Individual bucket seats have form-fitting foam rubber cushions. The floor is covered in soft carpeting, backed by sponge rubber. Large poçkets and ash trays in doors also serve as arm rests. Beautifully balanced instrument panel includes key-turn starter, electric clock, tachometer, hooded radio speaker.

POTENT "BLUE-FLAME" 6 engine, with three side-draft carburetors, 8 to 1 compression ratio, and overhead valves, puts a flashing 155 horsepower under the throttle. It has a dual exhaust system, efficient cooling and lubrication, and a shielded electrical system . . . plus Chevrolet's traditional six-cylinder economy of operation and maintenance.

Im Modelljahr 1954 gab es die Corvette auch mit einem V8-Motor; ein Jahr später erhielt der Wagen Kurbelscheiben in den Türen und – auf Wunsch – ein Hardtop. Der Wagen begann für die Amerikaner interessant zu werden.

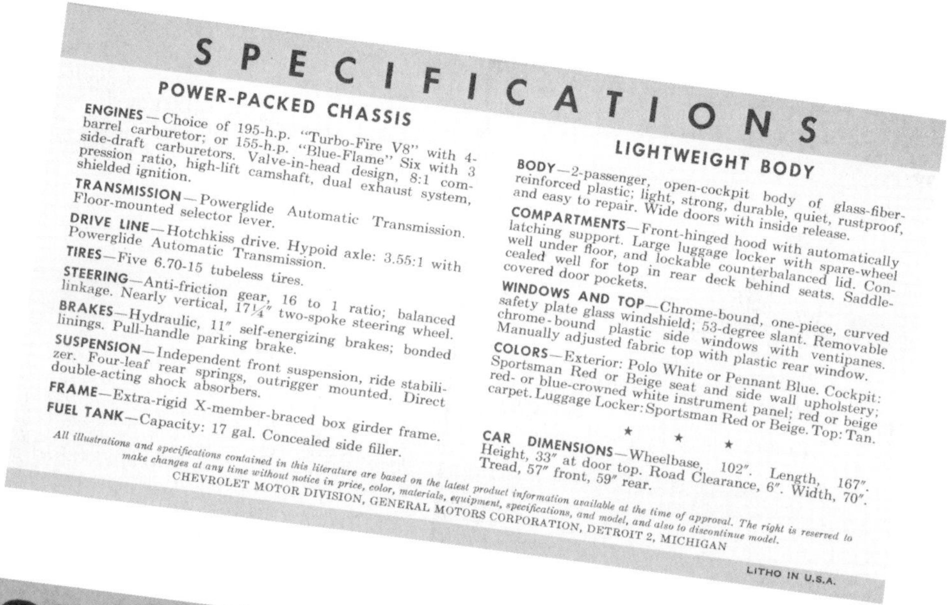

SPECIFICATIONS

POWER-PACKED CHASSIS

ENGINES—Choice of 195-h.p. "Turbo-Fire V8" with 4-barrel carburetor; or 155-h.p. "Blue-Flame" Six with 3 side-draft carburetors. Valve-in-head design, 8:1 compression ratio, high-lift camshaft, dual exhaust system, shielded ignition.

TRANSMISSION—Powerglide Automatic Transmission. Floor-mounted selector lever.

DRIVE LINE—Hotchkiss drive. Hypoid axle: 3.55:1 with Powerglide Automatic Transmission.

TIRES—Five 6.70-15 tubeless tires.

STEERING—Anti-friction gear, 16 to 1 ratio; balanced linkage. Nearly vertical, 17¼" two-spoke steering wheel.

BRAKES—Hydraulic, 11" self-energizing brakes; bonded linings. Pull-handle parking brake.

SUSPENSION—Independent front suspension, ride stabilizer. Four-leaf rear springs, outrigger mounted. Direct double-acting shock absorbers.

FRAME—Extra-rigid X-member-braced box girder frame.

FUEL TANK—Capacity: 17 gal. Concealed side filler.

LIGHTWEIGHT BODY

BODY—2-passenger, open-cockpit body of glass-fiber-reinforced plastic; light, strong, durable, quiet, rustproof, and easy to repair. Wide doors with inside release.

COMPARTMENTS—Front-hinged hood with automatically latching support. Large luggage locker with spare-wheel well under floor, and lockable counterbalanced lid. Concealed well for top in rear deck behind seats. Saddle-covered door pockets.

WINDOWS AND TOP—Chrome-bound, one-piece, curved safety plate glass windshield; 53-degree slant. Removable chrome-bound plastic side windows with ventipanes. Manually adjusted fabric top with plastic rear window.

COLORS—Exterior: Polo White or Pennant Blue. Cockpit: Sportsman Red or Beige seat and side wall upholstery; red- or blue-crowned white instrument panel; red or beige carpet. Luggage Locker: Sportsman Red or Beige. Top: Tan.

★ ★ ★

CAR DIMENSIONS—Wheelbase, 102". Length, 167". Height, 33" at door top. Road Clearance, 6". Width, 70". Tread, 57" front, 59" rear.

All illustrations and specifications contained in this literature are based on the latest product information available at the time of approval. The right is reserved to make changes at any time without notice in price, color, materials, equipment, specifications, and model, and also to discontinue model.

CHEVROLET MOTOR DIVISION, GENERAL MOTORS CORPORATION, DETROIT 2, MICHIGAN

LITHO IN U.S.A.

Links und rechts: Ein kleines Karton-Faltblatt von 1955, zweifarbig und ohne Übertreibungen. Als besonders sportlich galten Steinschlaggitter vor den Scheinwerfern.

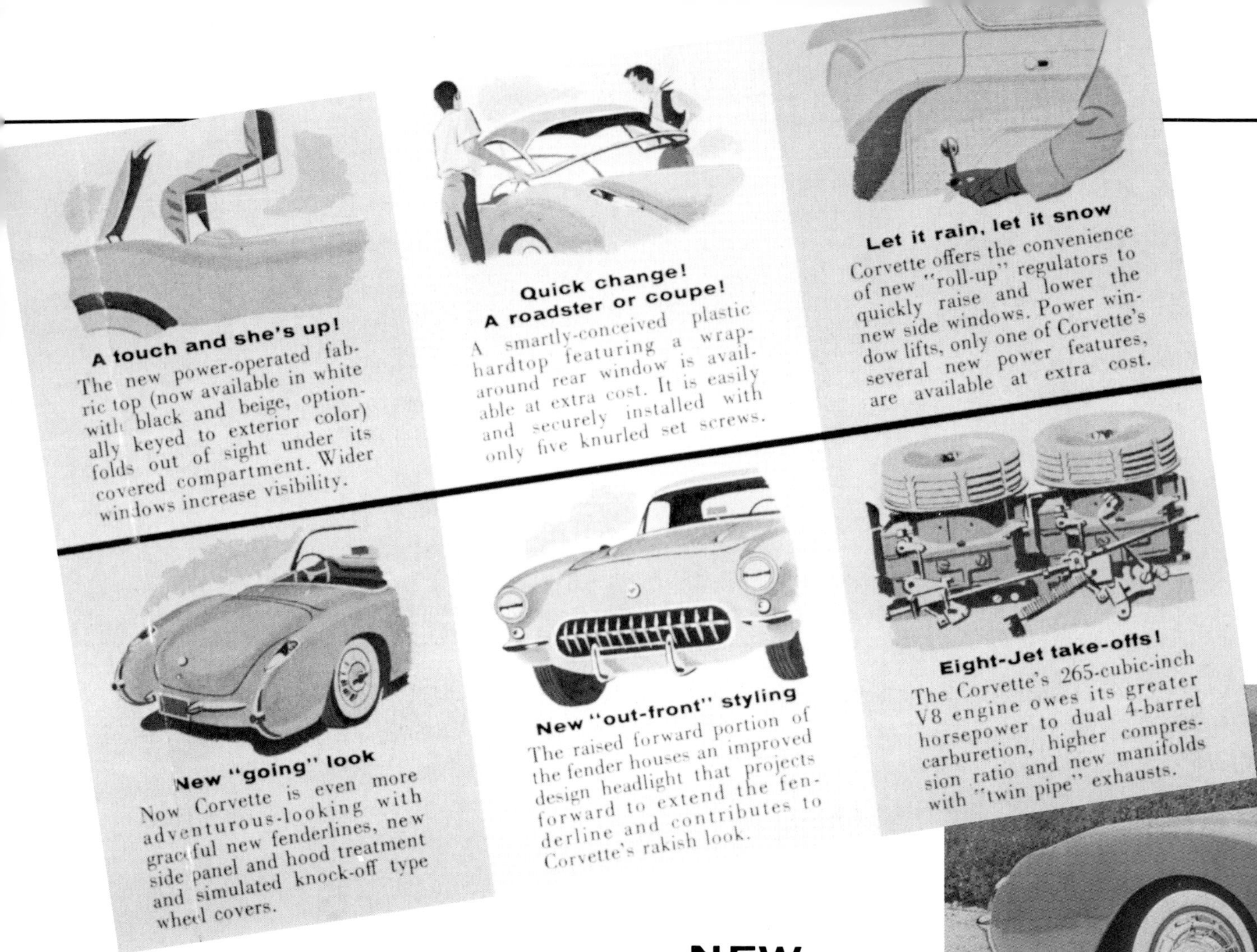

NEW

Corvette

Ähnlich aufgemacht wie der auf Seite 14/15 gezeigte Prospekt war dieses Faltblatt. Nur: Die Steinschlaggitter sind verschwunden, und die Flanken ziert eine kurvige Sicke. Die '56er Corvette ist attraktiv geworden . . .

SPECIFICATIONS

ENGINE

"Turbo-Fire Special V8." Valve-in-head design, 265-cubic-inch displacement, 3.75″ bore x 3.0″ stroke, 9.25:1 compression ratio. 225 horsepower at 5200 rpm. Torque 270 foot-pounds at 3600 rpm. Special high-lift camshaft, high-speed valve mechanism. Polished aluminum rocker covers. Dual four-barrel carburetion, buff aluminum racing-type air cleaners, special intake manifold. Full pressure lubrication system with full-flow oil filter.* High-power exhaust headers and full dual exhaust system. Shielded ignition, 12-volt electrical system. Engine precision balanced after assembly.

TRANSMISSION

Choice of special high-performance 3-speed close-ratio Synchro-Mesh (2.2:1 low and reverse, 1.31:1 second, 1.1 high) with high-capacity 10-inch coil-spring clutch, or optional Powerglide special automatic transmission.* Floor mounted gear or range selector.

REAR AXLE

High torque capacity axle; 3.55:1 ratio standard, 3.27:1 ratio optional with either Synchro-Mesh or Powerglide.

CHASSIS

Extra-rigid X-member-braced box girder frame. Independent coil front suspension with ride stabilizer. Self-lubricating four-leaf rear springs, outrigger mounted. Direct double-acting shock absorbers. Full anti-friction 16:1 ratio steering gear, balanced linkage. Competition-type steering wheel with three shock absorbing spring-steel spokes. Hydraulic 11-inch self-energizing brakes with new bonded linings, pull-handle parking brake. Suspended brake pedal. Choice of black or white sidewall* standard 6.70-15-4 ply tubeless tires or optional 6.70-15-4 ply high-speed nylon racing type.* Decorative wheel covers with simulated knock-off knobs. 17-gallon fuel tank with concealed side filler.

BODY FEATURES

Glass-fiber-reinforced plastic with sculptured side panels; light, strong, durable, quiet, rustproof, easy to repair. Distinctive embossed hood, front hinged, with automatic support, inside release. Simulated twin fender air scoops. Two-passenger compartment, large luggage locker with spare-wheel well under floor, concealed top well behind seats. Unique Corvette crossed-flag emblems on hood and trunk lid. Twin exhaust ports integral with rear bumpers. Chrome-bound, one-piece, curved safety plate glass windshield. Power-operated fabric top with wide plastic rear window. Richly trimmed quick-change hardtop* with rear-quarter windows and full-vision rear window.

INTERIOR FEATURES

Form-fitting vinyl-covered seats, individually adjustable, with safety belt.* Wide doors with built-in arm rest, push-button door handle, key lock, inside door release, swing-out door hinges. Choice of crank-operated or power* window lifts. Ash tray and glove compartment between seats; padded roll on instrument panel and doors, rubber-backed carpeting, metal door kick panels, sills, and step plates. Signal-seeking radio,* heater,* directional signals, electric clock, cigarette lighter, tachometer, outside and inside rear-view mirror, windshield washer.*

COLORS

Onyx Black with Red interior and Black or White top, Venetian Red with Red interior and Beige or White top, Cascade Green with Beige interior and Beige or White top, Aztec copper with Beige interior and Beige or White top, Arctic Blue with Beige or Red interior and Beige or White top, Polo White with Red interior and White or Black top.

DIMENSIONS

Wheelbase, 102″. Length, 168.01″. Overall height: top down, 49.20″; Convertible top, 51.09″; hardtop, 50.98″. Height at door 32.55″. Road clearance 6″. Width, 70.46″. Tread, 57″ front, 59″ rear.

*Optional at extra cost.

All illustrations and specifications contained in this literature are based on the latest information available at the time of publication approval. The right is reserved to make changes at any time without notice in price, color, materials, equipment and specifications.

CHEVROLET MOTOR DIVISION • GENERAL MOTORS CORPORATION • DETROIT 2, MICHIGAN

LITHO IN U.S.A.

wn convertible" and will accept nothing less than an
thentic, competition-type sports car will quickly sense
at *action* is the keynote of the new Corvette V8. But
nvenience is accented too, and you will find many
xury features seldom available in a car of this caliber.

Live, Lithe, Luxurious Action

Die technischen Daten des Modells 1956. Die Vielfalt der Karosserie-Farben ist beachtlich!

Ein Prospekt vom Sommer 1956, jetzt im Vierfarbdruck und mit einer Fülle interessanter Detailfotos. Vieles ist an der Corvette neu – siehe unten.

Close-up details reveal *New* Corvette Advancements

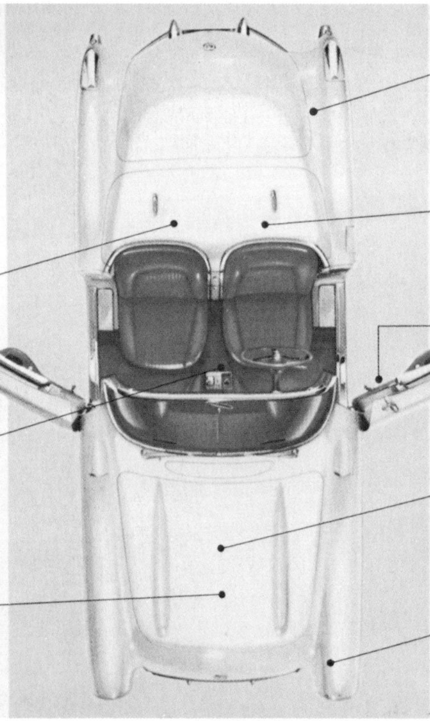

A touch . . . and she's up!

The new power-operated fabric top (now available in white with black and beige keyed to exterior color) folds out of sight under its plastic-lidded compartment behind the seat. Wider rear window and new-design side windows increase visibility.

This . . . is for the "Box Boys"

The new Corvette with a new floor-mounted "stick" shift close ratio Synchro-Mesh transmission. Here is the split-second up-shifting, down-shifting, close-ratio gear control demanded by the experts!

Eight-Jet Carburetion for take-offs!

The Corvette's 265-cubic-inch V8 engine owes its greater horsepower to dual 4-barrel carburetion, higher compression ratio and new manifolds with "twin pipe" exhausts.

Avant-Garde styling with a touch of tradition

The Corvette is a true sports car—not a scaled-down convertible. Now it's even more adventurous-looking with graceful new fender lines, new side panel and hood treatment and simulated knock-off type wheel covers.

Quick change! A roadster or coupe!

A plastic hardtop featuring a wraparound rear window is available as extra cost equipment. It is easily and securely installed with only five knurled set screws.

Let it rain, let it snow!

Corvette offers the convenience of roll-up regulators that quickly raise and lower the new windows. Power window lifts are available as an extra cost option.

A hood full of "Horses" add a carload of Safety!

The new "Turbo-fire V8" engine is a real life-saver when only sheer *passing power* can leave hazards behind and whisk you to safety. New cylinder heads up Corvette's compression ratio to 9.25 to 1!

"Out-front" styling for looking ahead

The raised-forward portion of the fender houses an improved design headlight that projects forward to extend the fender-line and contribute to Corvette's rakish look.

Das Titelblatt dieses Prospektes verheißt Tempo, doch eine Angabe zur Höchstgeschwindigkeit findet man nicht. Es genügte, von „high speed racing type tires" und den vielen PS zu sprechen . . .

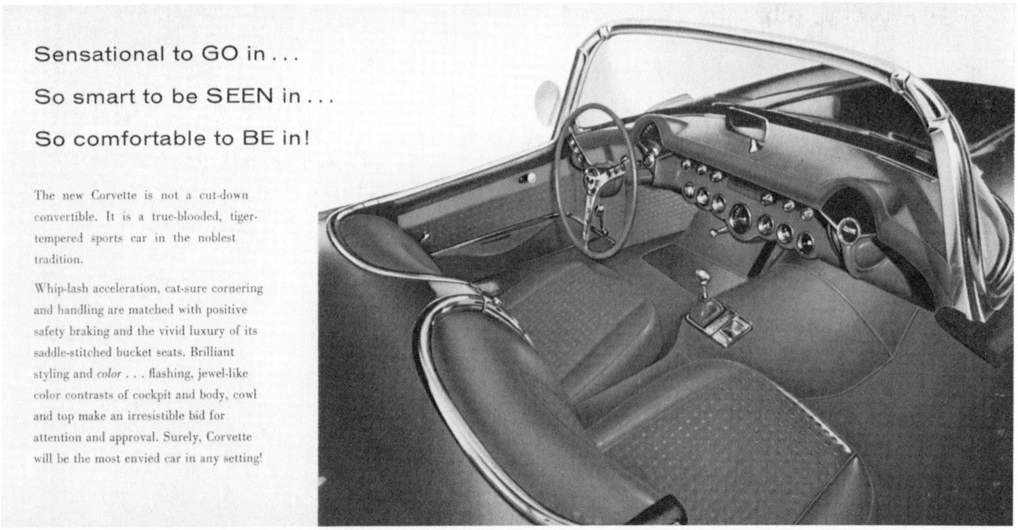

Fuel Injection: Ein PS pro Kubikzoll

1957 präsentierte sich die Corvette mit Einspritzmotor. Es gab den V8 in zwei Varianten – mit 250 und mit 283 PS. Zugleich offerierte man ein Viergang-Getriebe mit Handschaltung. Eine neue Ära in der Geschichte des „einzigen amerikanischen Sportwagens" begann.

Unten: Aus der Sammlung des Schülers Ralph Brown stammt dieser 1957er Prospekt. Er enthält erstmals Angaben zum neuen Einspritzmotor.

Rechts: Titelblatt eines 1959er Prospektes. Die Abbildungen werden flotter, die Umsatzzahlen besser.

1959
Chevrolet
CORVETTE
AMERICA'S
SPORTS CAR

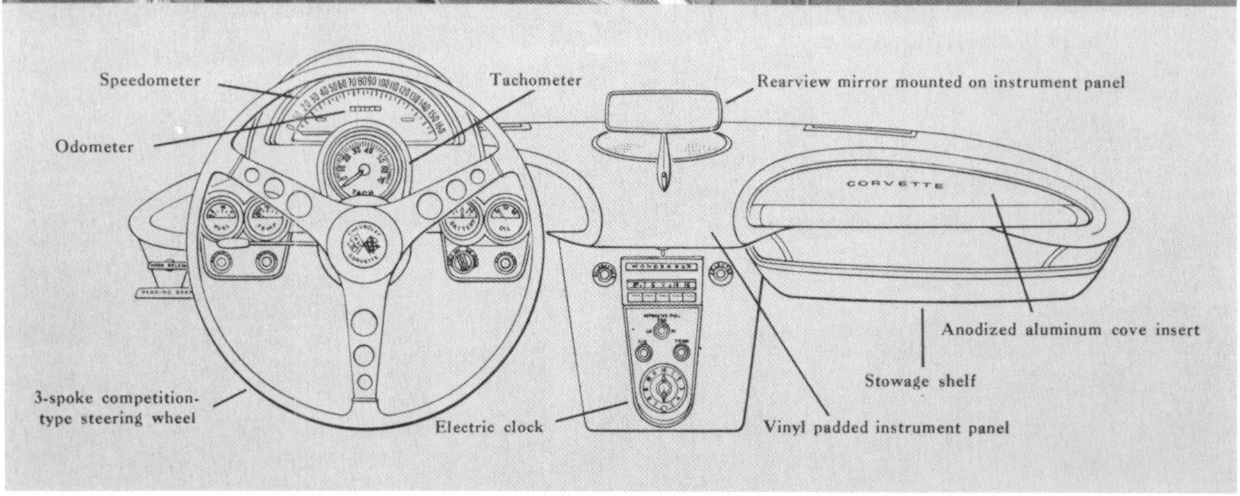
Speedometer
Tachometer
Rearview mirror mounted on instrument panel
Odometer
CORVETTE
Anodized aluminum cove insert
Stowage shelf
3-spoke competition-
type steering wheel
Electric clock
Vinyl padded instrument panel

Links Interieur 1959, rechts ein Prospekt von 1960.

Bilder einer Teststrecke enthält dieser Corvette-Prospekt von 1961. Beschleunigungs- oder andere „Speed"-Werte enthält auch er nicht. Worauf es dem Käufer ankam, läßt er dennoch deutlich erkennen. Die Gentlemen im Wagen müssen viel Spaß gehabt haben . . .

1961

1962

Oben: Der erste Sting Ray-Prospekt aus dem Jahre 1963. Motoren bis 360 PS sind lieferbar!

FUEL
WATER TEMP
OIL
LIGHTS
BATTERY
HEADLIGHTS
Corvette
Sting Ray

Links: Bemerkenswert aufgeräumt geht es nun im Cockpit der Corvette zu (1965).

Oben: Kurze Rückblende auf das Modelljahr 1962. Ein junges Traumpaar demonstriert auf bunten Seiten, wie schön das Leben an Bord der Corvette sein kann.

Mit dem Stachelrochen zu neuen Ufern 1963

Der Sting Ray (Stachelrochen) war wesentlich kantiger im Karosserie-Design als sein Vorgänger. Aber der neue Stil – eine Kreation Bill Mitchells – kam gut an. 10 919 Cabriolets und 10 594 Coupés wurden vom Modell-Jahrgang 1963 produziert. Später gab es allerdings eine deutliche Bevorzugung des offenen Wagens.

Werbung für den Sting Ray 1963. Man bekommt den Wagen als Fastback-Coupé, als Cabrio mit Soft- oder mit Hardtop. Der Designer Arkus-Duntov kam mit dem neuen Styling den Vorstellungen vieler Amerikaner von einem modernen Sportwagen nahe.

Shown on Cover: Corvette Sting Ray Sport Coupe in Riverside Red

Corvette Sting Ray Convertible in Riverside Red

NEW GRACE AND ELEGANCE SILHOUETTE AMERICA'S SPORTS CAR

Corvette steps out smartly with an exhilarating new look for '63. A freshly elegant look that promises to lift the spirits of any buff who takes the wheel. It's the Corvette Sting Ray! Two sparkling new models, both pointing the way to a classic new concept in American sports car design.

Catch an eyeful of the Corvette newcomer, the exciting Sport Coupe. Graceful body panels and compound-curved side windows emphasize the miles-ahead aerodynamic design. Power-operated, retractable headlamps rotate out of sight to blend into the unobstructed hood line. Doors extend upward into the roof, adding armchair ease and comfort to sliding in and out. This is the Corvette Sting Ray Sport Coupe. Clean, taut, fresh in every detail.

You'll find the Convertible is jauntier than ever in '63. Uncluttered lines accented front and rear by trim wrap-around bumpers. The subtle contour of the smoothly molded rear deck. A gleaming aluminum grille, retractable head-lamps and a sweeping hood-length windsplit. Top up or down, graceful streamlining is the goal. And the Corvette Sting Ray Convertible achieves it.

SURE-FOOTED CONFIDENCE ON THE TOUGHEST TRAILS

Two chassis innovations take much of the credit for the new Corvette's firm level ride, precise handling and maneuverability: a shorter 98" wheelbase and a unique rear suspension and newly designed rear axle. The rear suspension features a three-link independent system at each wheel. A radius arm running from the frame to the rear spindle support, a control rod attached to the differential and wheel spindle, and the double universal-jointed tubular axle shaft combine to provide nearly vertical wheel movement. One multi-leaf transverse spring (bolted to the differential carrier) extends from rear wheel to rear wheel and takes only vertical suspension loads. Braking, acceleration and lateral forces are transmitted by the radius arms, axles and control rods to the differential and the frame. The differential assembly is attached to the frame by a bolted-in crossmember; large rubber cups serve to dampen driveline vibrations. Small movements of the differential are taken up by universal joints on the one-piece propeller shaft. Corvette's new rear suspension in combination with improved coil-spring spherical joint front suspension produces better traction, a stable ride and excellent handling. You can add to tire and handling stability with Corvette's optional wide-rim cast aluminum wheels*. Vented-fin design for cooling; knock-off hubs for quick, simple wheel and tire changing.

For increased rigidity and protection, the Convertible has a steel framework surrounding the passenger compartment, while the Sport Coupe has overhead steel roof members as well.

Optional Aluminum Wheels with Knock-off Hubs.*

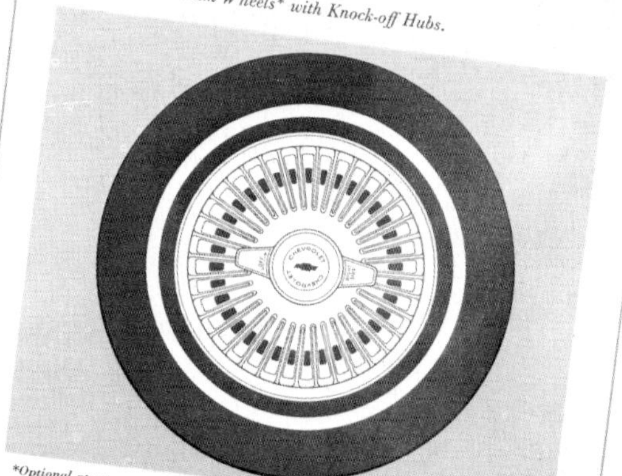

**Optional at extra cost.*

Leichtmetallfelgen mit Zentralverschluß – der letzte Schrei. Mit verkürztem Radstand und neuer Hinterachse verspricht G.M. ein völlig neues Fahrgefühl. Rechts: Erster 1965er Prospekt.

1965
CORVETTE
STING RAY
CORVETTE

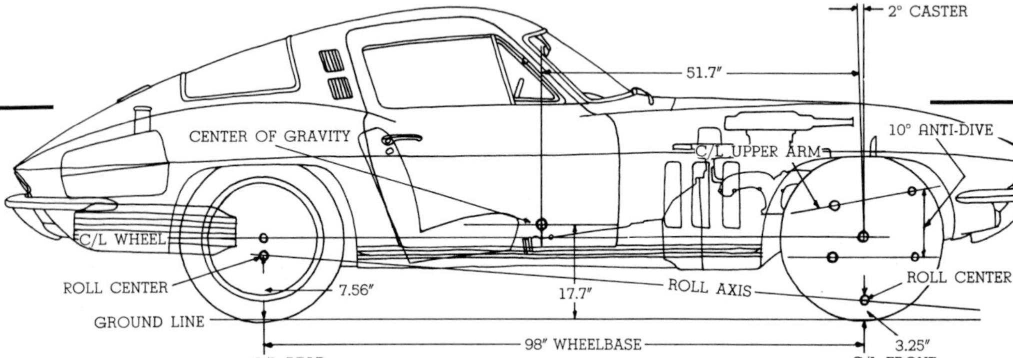

Suspension geometry at design weight

DESIGN CONCEPT: The key to Sting Ray's roadability and handling lies in its 4-wheel independent suspension and its greater rearward weight distribution. Chevrolet engineers chose the fully independent suspension so that optimum use could be made of the great power available. The rearward weight distribution makes it possible to achieve excellent handling and still maintain an acceptably gentle ride. The major vehicle masses — the heavier components of the Sting Ray—are located so that the suspension and steering systems can work with the design, rather than having to compensate for imbalance. The Sting Ray has been basically *right* from its original concept. Constant refinement and continual development have gone forward to make the 1965 Corvette Sting Ray more than ever one of the most deeply satisfying driving experiences available in the world.

EXTRA-COST OPTIONAL EQUIPMENT

The following equipment, shown previously in illustrations or described in the text, is available at extra cost for the Corvette Sting Ray. These options add driving pleasure, or prepare the car for special uses. They allow the Sting Ray owner to equip his car to his own particular tastes.

CHASSIS: Heavy-duty suspension. (Rear spring rate: 305 lb./in. Rear shock absorbers: 1⅜ in. Front spring rate: 550 lb./in. Front shock absorbers: recalibrated. Stabilizer bar: 0.94-inch diameter.) Positraction; power brakes; telescopic steering column; power steering; optional axle ratio; nylon tires; whitewall tires; cast aluminum wheels with wide-base six-inch rims and knock-off hubs.

ENGINE: Off-road service exhaust system; exposed, side-mounted exhaust system; 36-gallon fuel tank (Sport Coupe only). (Note: when 36-gallon fuel tank is fitted, luggage compartment is partially carpeted); transistor ignition and voltage regulator; 300-horsepower engine; 350-horsepower engine; 365-horsepower engine; 375-horsepower Ramjet Fuel Injection engine.

TRANSMISSION: 4-Speed; 4-Speed close ratio; Powerglide.

BODY: Soft-Ray tinted glass; back-up lights and non-glare inside rear-view mirror; Four-Season air conditioning; genuine leather seat upholstery; wood-rimmed steering wheel; electric windows; AM/FM pushbutton radio with remote control power antenna; removeable hard top. (Convertible only. You can, however, specify either hard top or soft top at no extra cost—or order both with hard top at extra cost.)

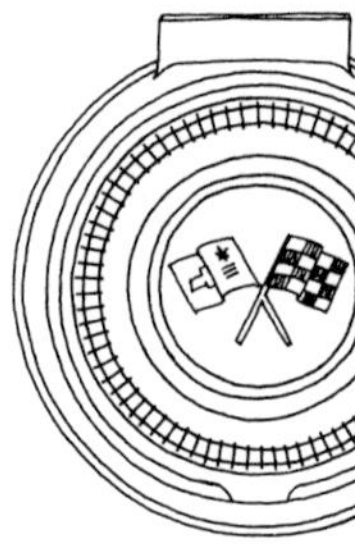

Gas filler door emblem

from rubber to roof, a sports car...

for performance -and style-minded individuals.

Bilder aus einem 1965er Prospekt. Er enthält ausgezeichnete Fotos und detaillierte Zeichnungen.

CORVETTE

CORVETTE

Die Karosserie der '65er Corvette besteht laut Katalog aus 31 Kunststoff-Teilen. Rechts: Abbildung aus einem '66er Prospekt.

The sport coupe's fully carpeted luggage area

Right: Enthusiast's delight: 4-Speed box

Seat belts with retractors are standard

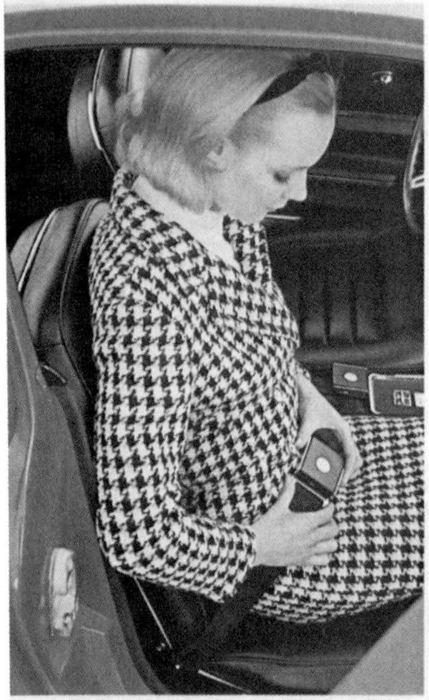

Pushbutton AM/FM all-transistor radio

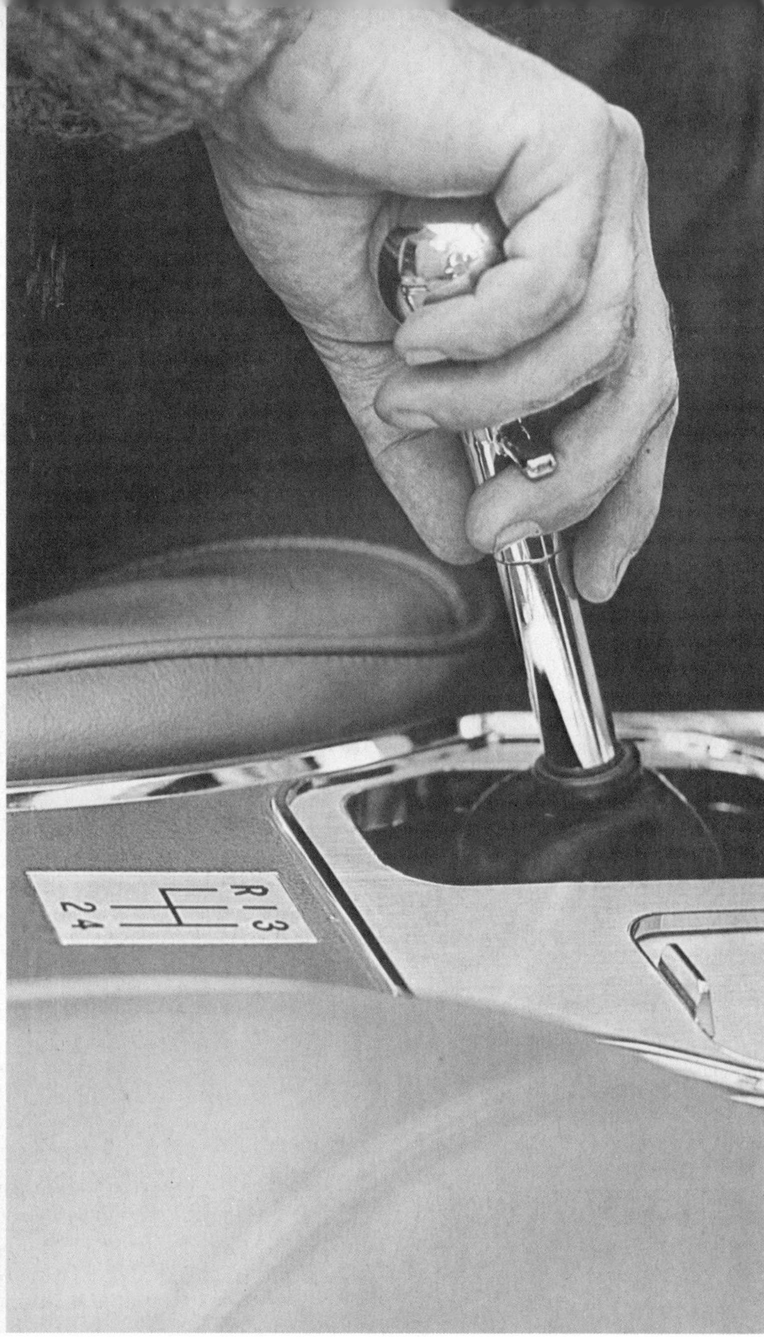

Als sportlich galt die Handschaltung, aber man erhielt auf Wunsch auch eine Automatik. Mit Zweipunkt-Gurten gab man sich indes noch immer zufrieden.

CORVETTE

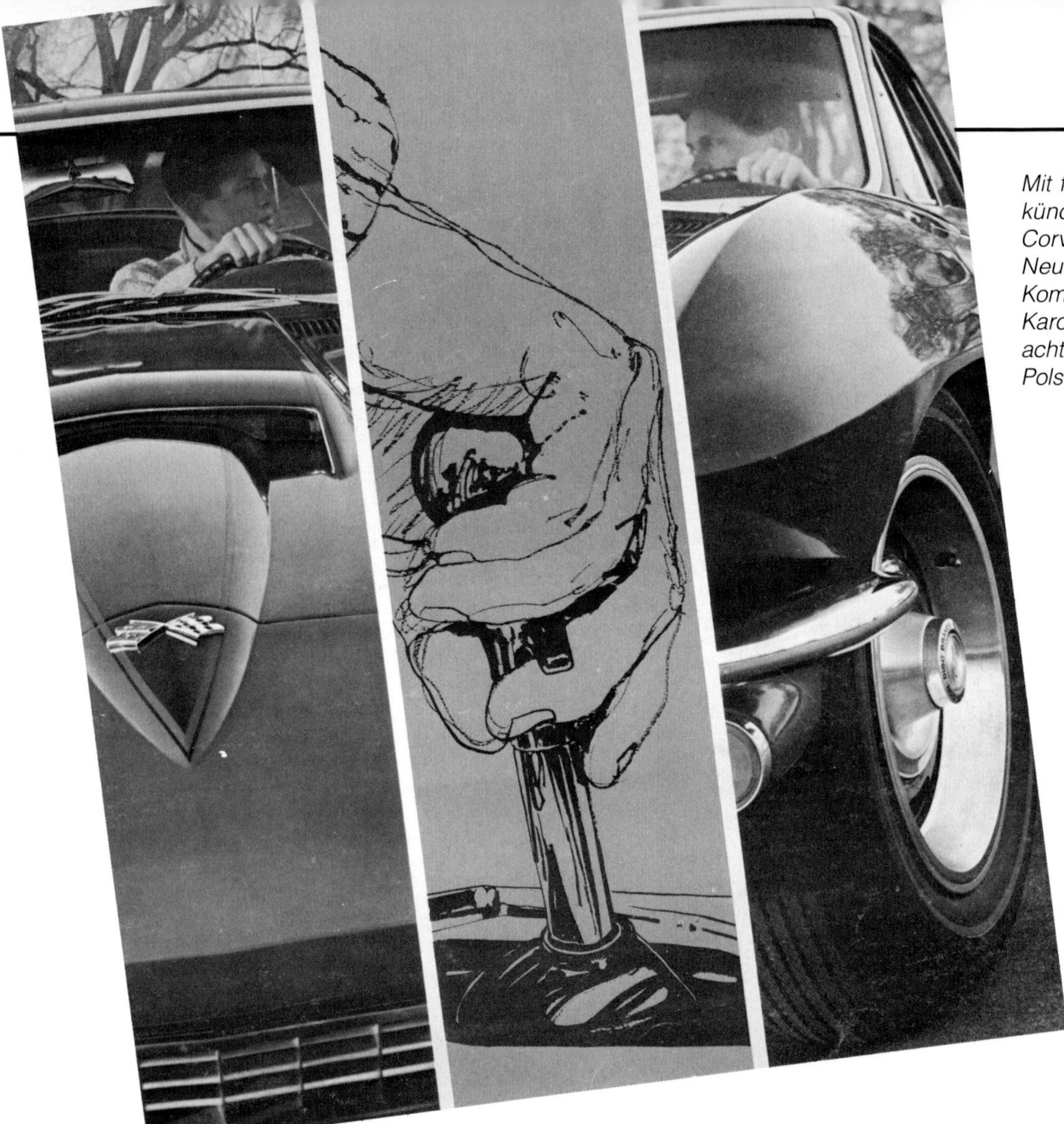

Mit flotten Zeichnungen kündigt dieser '67er Corvette-Prospekt die Neuerungen an. Eine Kombination von zehn Karosseriefarben und acht Varianten der Polsterung wird offeriert.

'67 Corvette
BY CHEVROLET

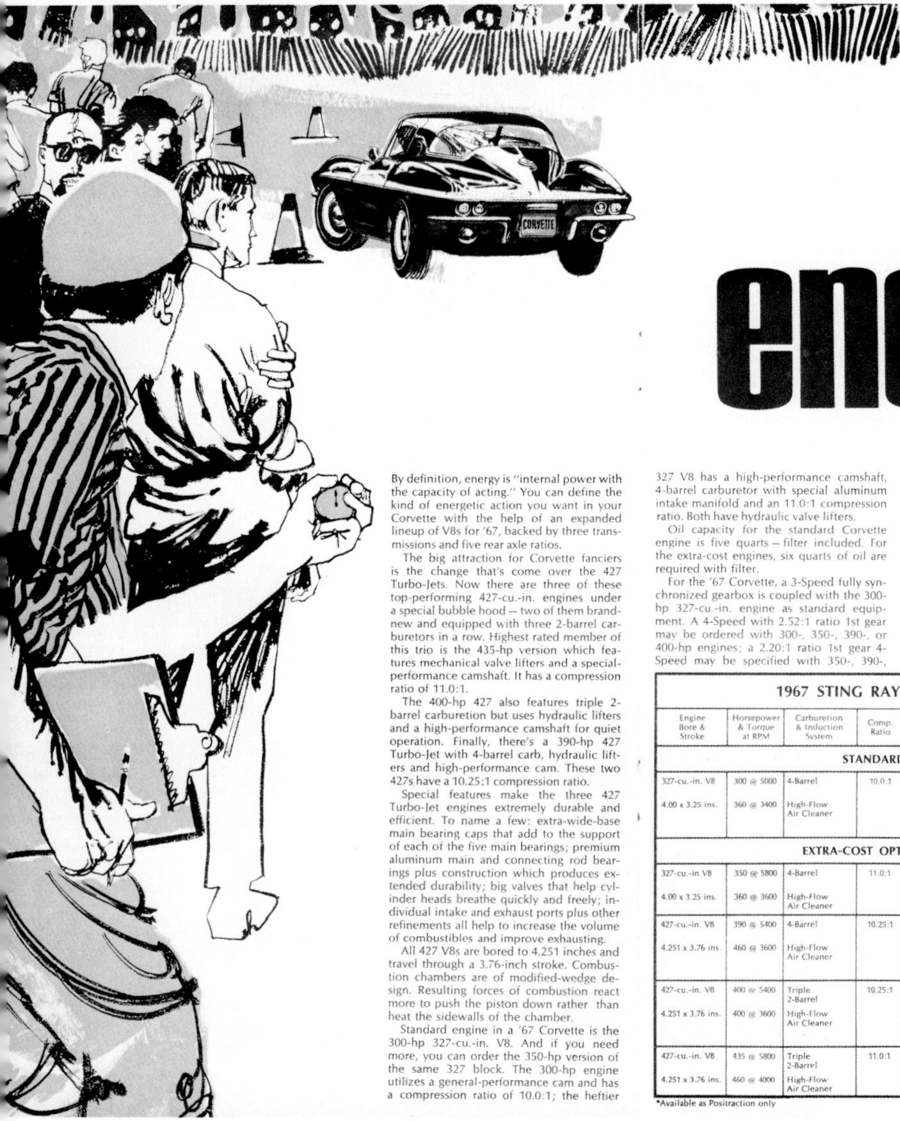

energetic

By definition, energy is "internal power with the capacity of acting." You can define the kind of energetic action you want in your Corvette with the help of an expanded lineup of V8s for '67, backed by three transmissions and five rear axle ratios.

The big attraction for Corvette fanciers is the change that's come over the 427 Turbo-Jets. Now there are three of these top-performing 427-cu.-in. engines under a special bubble hood — two of them brand-new and equipped with three 2-barrel carburetors in a row. Highest rated member of this trio is the 435-hp version which features mechanical valve lifters and a special-performance camshaft. It has a compression ratio of 11.0:1.

The 400-hp 427 also features triple 2-barrel carburetion but uses hydraulic lifters and a high-performance camshaft for quiet operation. Finally, there's a 390-hp 427 Turbo-Jet with 4-barrel carb, hydraulic lifters and high-performance cam. These two 427s have a 10.25:1 compression ratio.

Special features make the three 427 Turbo-Jet engines extremely durable and efficient. To name a few: extra-wide-base main bearing caps that add to the support of each of the five main bearings; premium aluminum main and connecting rod bearings plus construction which produces extended durability; big valves that help cylinder heads breathe quickly and freely; individual intake and exhaust ports plus other refinements all help to increase the volume of combustibles and improve exhausting.

All 427 V8s are bored to 4.251 inches and travel through a 3.76-inch stroke. Combustion chambers are of modified-wedge design. Resulting forces of combustion react more to push the piston down rather than heat the sidewalls of the chamber.

Standard engine in a '67 Corvette is the 300-hp 327-cu.-in. V8. And if you need more, you can order the 350-hp version of the same 327 block. The 300-hp engine utilizes a general-performance cam and has a compression ratio of 10.0:1; the heftier 327 V8 has a high-performance camshaft, 4-barrel carburetor with special aluminum intake manifold and an 11.0:1 compression ratio. Both have hydraulic valve lifters.

Oil capacity for the standard Corvette engine is five quarts — filter included. For the extra-cost engines, six quarts of oil are required with filter.

For the '67 Corvette, a 3-Speed fully synchronized gearbox is coupled with the 300-hp 327-cu.-in. engine as standard equipment. A 4-Speed with 2.52:1 ratio 1st gear may be ordered with 300-, 350-, 390-, or 400-hp engines; a 2.20:1 ratio 1st gear 4-Speed may be specified with 350-, 390-, 400-, and 435-hp V8s. This year, for more leisure-minded sports car buffs, Powerglide automatic transmission can be ordered with the 300-, 390-, and 400-hp engines.

Five rear axle ratios are available, depending on the engine you select, to provide you with smooth going or rugged performance. A Positraction rear axle, which can be specified with any Corvette ratio, routes engine power to the rear wheel with the greatest traction. This is especially valuable on muddy, slippery or other irregular surfaces, in sand and snow. Check the axle ratio chart at right to determine rate of speed with various axle ratios.

1967 STING RAY POWER TEAMS

Engine Bore & Stroke	Horsepower & Torque at RPM	Carburetion & Induction System	Comp. Ratio	Cam & Lifters	Transmissions	Axle Ratios	
						Standard	Positraction
STANDARD ENGINE							
327-cu.-in. V8 4.00 x 3.25 ins.	300 @ 5000 360 @ 3400	4-Barrel High-Flow Air Cleaner	10.0:1	General Performance Hydraulic	3-Speed (2.54:1 Low)	3.36:1	3.08:1 3.36:1
					4-Speed (2.52:1 Low)	3.36:1	3.08:1 3.36:1
					Powerglide	3.36:1	3.36:1
EXTRA-COST OPTIONAL ENGINES							
327-cu.-in V8 4.00 x 3.25 ins.	350 @ 5800 360 @ 3600	4-Barrel High-Flow Air Cleaner	11.0:1	High Performance Hydraulic	4-Speed (2.52:1 Low)	3.36:1	3.36:1 3.55:1
					4-Speed (2.20:1 Low)	3.70:1	3.70:1 4.11:1
427-cu.-in. V8 4.251 x 3.76 ins.	390 @ 5400 460 @ 3600	4-Barrel High-Flow Air Cleaner	10.25:1	High Performance Hydraulic	4-Speed (2.52:1 Low)	3.08:1*	3.36:1
					4-Speed (2.20:1 Low)	3.36:1*	3.08:1 3.55:1
					Powerglide	3.36:1*	3.70:1
427-cu.-in. V8 4.251 x 3.76 ins.	400 @ 5400 400 @ 3600	Triple 2-Barrel High-Flow Air Cleaner	10.25:1	High Performance Hydraulic	4-Speed (2.52:1 Low)	3.08:1*	3.36:1
					4-Speed (2.20:1 Low) Powerglide	3.36:1*	3.08:1 3.55:1 3.70:1
427-cu.-in. V8 4.251 x 3.76 ins.	435 @ 5800 460 @ 4000	Triple 2-Barrel High-Flow Air Cleaner	11.0:1	Special Performance Mechanical	4-Speed (2.20:1 Low)	3.55:1*	3.36:1* 3.70:1* 4.11:1*

*Available as Positraction only

MILES PER HOUR PER 1000 ENGINE RPM IN FINAL DRIVE

(Figures are estimated without allowance for tire expansion or slippage.)

3.08:1 = 25.6 3.36:1 = 23.1
3.55:1 = 22.2 3.70:1 = 21.3
4.11:1 = 19.2

Try a '67 Corvette as soon as you can. You'll find there's no energy wasted.

EXTRA-COST OPTIONS AND CUSTOM FEATURES* TO MAKE DRIVING A CORVETTE EVEN MORE PLEASURABLE

350-hp Turbo-Fire 327; 390-, 400- or 435-hp Turbo-Jet 427. An automatic Powerglide or 4-Speed fully synchronized transmission. Four-Season air conditioning. Power brakes, power steering, power windows. AM/FM pushbutton radio. Removable hardtop for convertible. Black vinyl roof cover for removable hardtop. Positraction rear axle. Leather seat trim. Shoulder belts. Whitewall or red-stripe tires. Soft-Ray tinted windows and/or windshield. Full-transistor ignition system (not available with standard engine). Heavy-duty brakes. Special-performance front and rear suspension. Off-road exhaust system (not available with Powerglide). Dual side-mounted off-road exhausts. Telescopic steering wheel. Emergency road kit. Compass. Gas tank filler cap lock. Removable floor mats. 36.5-gallon gas tank for sport coupe only. Convertible deck lid luggage carrier plus strap. Convertible deck lid ski rack. Strato-ease headrests. Speed warning unit. Portable hand spotlight. Special cast-aluminum wheels.

*Check your Chevrolet dealer for these and other extra-cost items along with their model application and availability with other equipment.

9

Motorvarianten, die keine Wünsche offen ließen, und dementsprechende Getriebe- und Hinterachs-Abstufungen. Die Aufpreise bewegten sich für derlei Extras in zivilen Bereichen . . .

CORVETTE

Links: *Titelseite des ersten Prospekts für das Modelljahr 1968. Der innen wie außen gänzlich überarbeitete Wagen wirkt extrem bullig, wenn nicht aggressiv. Dreipunktgurte sind im Coupé jetzt Standard.*

Hide-A-Way windshield wiper-washer system closed . . . and open.

For comfort, air flows through Corvette with full door windows closed, thanks to the new Astro Ventilation system with vent-ports in the driver and passenger sides of the instrument panel. For protection, there are safety features like never before (some are listed on page 11). For long-lasting good looks, choose from ten Magic-Mirror finishes. *Corvette '68 . . . all different all over.*

Rechts: *Neu sind auch viele Details wie die versenkten Scheibenwischer oder das Belüftungssystem. Die Presse ermittelte den Wagen als „The Best Allround Car" des Jahres – zum viertenmal. Die Abbildungen auf den nachfolgenden Seiten entstammen dem gleichen Prospekt.*

Corvette Sting Ray Coupe interior with high-back slim-tapered bucket seat.

Settle down!

The Corvette cockpit is made for the traveling duo. Thin tapered and contoured buckets are very comfortably high-backed. Supple all-vinyl upholstery is standard, or you can order genuine leather. Between the seats the center console houses the parking brake lever, gear shift, cigarette lighter and ashtray, thumb-wheel heater controls, air vent controls, and light monitoring system indicators (to check operation of important outside running lights from inside through space-age fiber optics). The console also stows seat belt buckle straps—twin sets with pushbutton buckles are standard. Coupe equipment also includes twin shoulder belts.

Riding just above the console is the recessed instrument cluster. Here's where the engine tale is told. Water temperature, oil pressure and fuel gauges along with an ammeter and rally clock are positioned for easy reading. Windshield wiper-washer controls are also in console. And if you order an AM/FM radio—available wit or without FM Stereo multiplex—controls are mounted here hor zontally. Joining in are new features like door ajar flasher an seat belt reminder light. Directly in front of the driver ar the speedometer, tachometer, trip odometer, light controls, ign tion lock, high beam indicator, turn signal indicator, brake syster warning light—and a 3-spoke steering wheel that looks like wooc

Luxurious deep-twist carpeting looks and feels great. It eve

Shown on cover: Corvette Sting Ray Coupe

Corvette Sting Ray Coupe with roof sections in place.

Go hardtop!

The Corvette Sting Ray is for those who appreciate the true sports kind of car – and even for those who don't right now. It's that special kind of an automobile that comes along about once every generation to totally arrest the imagination of car buffs. In 15 years of Corvettes the car has not only driven into prominence in the sports car field, but has also been a forerunner of some exciting and practical automobile innovation. For 1968, the mechanics of Sting Ray have been improved and refined (it's still basically made for people who feel that the best part of living is driving), and this, obviously, is a most inspiring year for design.

Consider: the '68 Sting Ray Coupe is a hardtop and more. Uncommon removable sections over pilot and navigator lift out for open air moving. A nearly vertical glass rear window tucks out of the way into a neat compartment in the luggage area. The effect is a flow-through cochère roof that's never been seen on an American production sports car until now.

Long, low profile with blunt styling brings up the rear per the continental GT tradition. The aerodynamic design features a spoiler back there, too. Behind front wheels, functional louvers help keep the horses cool. Wraparound front and rear bumpers plus line-smoothing hideaway features help make Corvette a trim one style-wise. On the nose end, vacuum-operated headlights glide open automatically when lights are turned on. Windshield wipers aren't around when they shouldn't be. They're hidden under a power-operated panel which actuates when

1969 CORVETTE
Putting you first, keeps us first
CHEVROLET

Titelblatt des Ankündigungsprospektes für 1969 und Interieuraufnahme. Studiotricks und brillante Close-ups wechseln sich ab (nachfolgende Seiten).

grabbing 15-inch wide ovals plus new 8-inch wide wheels and wider tread give Stingray a better grip . . . and an even bolder appearance. Other subtle but significant refinements include a stronger, more rigid frame for improved ride and handling, new maximum security 3-way locking system on the steering column and unique headlight washers that even clean in motion with jets of water.

Shown here are the ways you can get it: Coupe with removable hardtop sections; Convertible with soft top or removable hardtop. *For a more complete list of Corvette extra-cost Options and Custom Features illustrated or described throughout this book, see Page 11.*

Convertible with top down.

Vinyl-covered removable hardtop.

Headlight washers.

V8's in addition to the standard 300-hp V8. Prefer 4-Speed? You have a choice of gear ratios offered with all engines except the standard 300-hp and the 435-hp V8.

New Corvette power team features for '69 include new, larger 350 CID 300-hp engine as standard, or a 350-hp version is available, sturdier engine construction on the 350 CID, thicker bulkheads and main bearing caps, firmer crankshaft clamping with longer washer head bolts, extra-firm 4-bolt main bearing cap attachment and improved cooling system.

We even have a special engine (L-88) that we don't recommend for street use.

Transmissions: Standard 3-Speed fully synchronized; 4-Speed fully synchronized (wide-range or close-ratio); Turbo Hydra-Matic which operates automatically unless you want to shift it—through three forward ranges.

Of course, four-wheel disc brakes are still standard on Corvette—and in stopping ability, fade resistance and modulation they're very much appreciated by just about anybody interested in sports cars. Other features you get with Corvette include a new anti-interference ignition system, a high-output Delcotron generator, high-capacity energizer type battery, rustproof fiber glass body—and everything put together with a thoroughness and attention to detail that Corvette owners fully understand.

Standard equipment safety and security features on the 1969 Corvette include: energy-absorbing steering column □ seat belts with pushbutton buckles □ shoulder belts with inertia retractors (Coupe only) □ head restraints □ passenger-guard door locks □ safety door latches and hinges □ four-way hazard warning flasher □ dual master cylinder brake system with warning light and corrosion-resistant brake lines □ tire safety rims □ folding seat back latches □ dual-speed windshield wipers and washer □ dual-action safety hood latch □ outside rearview mirror □ back-up lights □ side marker lights and parking lights that illuminate with headlights □ energy-absorbing instrument panel □ padded sun visors □ reduced-glare instrument panel top, inside windshield mouldings, steering wheel hub and windshield wiper arms and blades □ wide inside day-night mirror with deflecting base □ lane-change feature in direction signal control □ safety armrests □ thick-laminate windshield □ soft, low-profile window control knobs □ smooth contoured door and window regulator handles □ anti-theft ignition key warning buzzer □ starter safety switch (to prevent engine starting when in gear) on all transmissions □ snag-resistant steering wheel hardware □ non-projecting wheel trim □ improved fuel tank retention □ headlight aiming access provision □ fail-safe concealed headlights □ anti-theft ignition, steering and transmission lock.

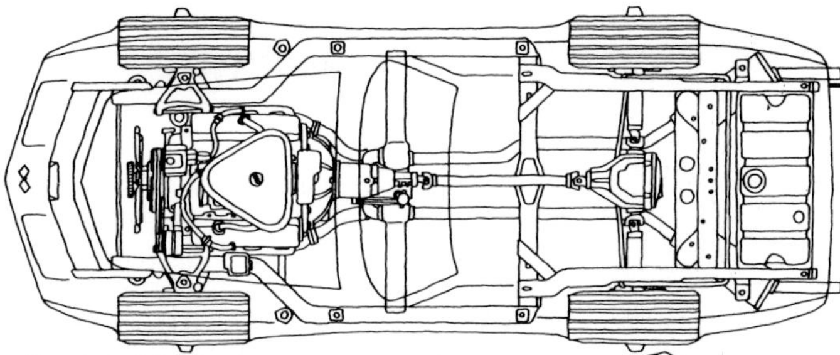

Top view of chassis.

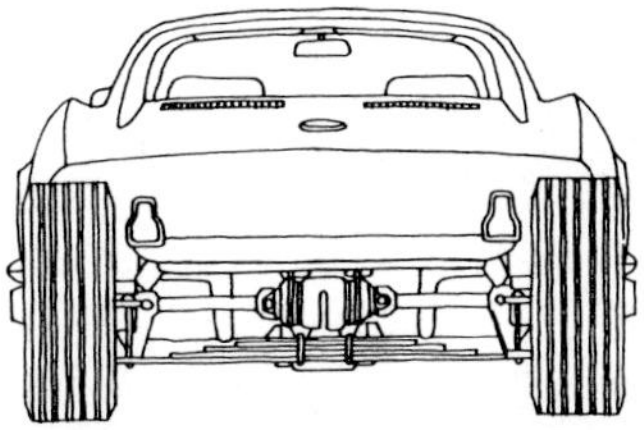

Fully independent rear suspension.

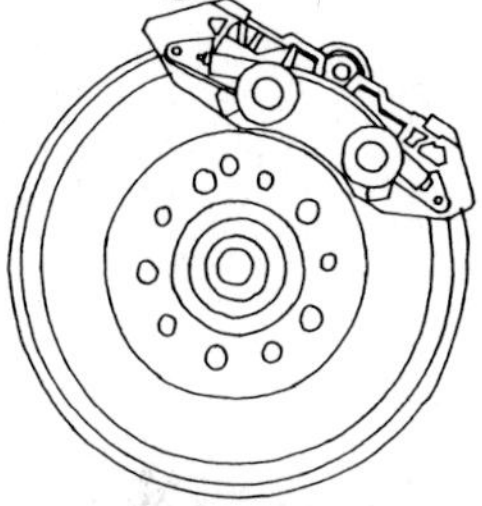

Advanced design disc brakes.

Engine	Transmission	Rear Axle Ratio (:1)							
		Without Air Cond.				With Air Cond.			
		Std	Optional			Std	Optional		
			Econ	Perf	Spcl		Econ	Perf	Spcl
BASE ENGINE									
300 HP Turbo-Fire 350 350-Cu.-In. V8	3-Speed (2.54:1 Low)	3.36 *	3.08 **			3.36 *	3.08 **		
	4-Speed (2.52:1 Low)								
	Turbo Hydra-Matic	3.08 **				3.08 **			
OPTIONAL ENGINES									
350 HP Turbo-Fire 350 350-Cu.-In. V8 RPO L46	4-Speed (2.52:1 Low)	3.36 *		3.55 **		3.36 *		3.55 **	
	4-Speed (2.20:1 Low)	3.70 *		4.11 **		3.70 *		4.11 **	
390 HP Turbo-Jet 427 427-Cu.-In. V8 RPO L36	4-Speed (2.52:1 Low)	3.08 **		3.36 **		3.08 **			
	4-Speed (2.20:1 Low)	3.36 **	3.08 **	3.55 **	3.70 **	Air Conditioning Not Available			
	Turbo Hydra-Matic	3.08 **	2.73 **			3.08 **	2.73 **		
400 HP Turbo-Jet 427 427-Cu.-In. V8 RPO L68	4-Speed (2.52:1 Low)	3.08 **		3.36 **		3.08 **			
	4-Speed (2.20:1 Low)	3.36 **	3.08 **	3.55 **	3.70 **	Air Conditioning Not Available			
	Turbo Hydra-Matic	3.08 **	2.73 **			3.08 **	2.73 **		
435 HP Turbo-Jet 427 427-Cu.-In. V8 RPO L71	4-Speed (2.20:1 Low)	3.55 **	3.36 **	3.70 **	4.11 **	Air Conditioning Not Available			
	Turbo Hydra-Matic	3.08 **	2.73 **	3.36 **					
SPECIAL HIGH PERFORMANCE ENGINE (OFF-ROAD APPLICATION ONLY)									
430 HP Turbo-Jet 427 427-Cu.-In. V8 RPO L88	H.D. 4-Speed (2.20:1 Low)	3.36 **	3.08 **	3.55 **	3.70 4.11 4.56 **	Air Conditioning Not Available			
	Turbo Hydra-Matic	3.08 **	2.73 **	3.36 **					

*Positraction available. **Positraction required.

Corvette Stingray Coupe
CHEVROLET
Litho in U.S.A.—D-67141
GM
MARK OF EXCELLENCE

Links: 1969er Werbung – mit viel Black Magic. Rechts: 1970 hieß es, man erhalte mehr als nur ein Auto, wenn man eine Corvette kaufe. Ob die Dame im Hintergrund gemeint war?

Mission Control Center '70.

Cape Kennedy hasn't got anything on us. Corvette's cockpit is as heavy on instrumentation as it is on comfort.

First, you sit yourself down in one of the high-backed contoured bucket seats featuring our new integrated head restraints. The shoulder belts (standard on coupe) are guided through a slot in each seatback for neat, secure positioning.

You rest your feet on soft carpeting that not only stretches wall to wall but over the entire rear stowage area with its hidden compartments for valuables, battery and tools.

You check out the central command console before your countdown. Tach, ammeter, water temp, oil pressure, fuel gauge, brake warning light, running light monitors—you name it, it's there.

Once under way, you can enjoy Astro Ventilation, which routes outside air in, through your choice of high or low vents. A rear deck vent exhausts stale air, for a constant flow, even with the windows closed.

New for '70 is a Custom Interior you can order with black or saddle leather seats, plush cut-pile carpeting and the rich look of wood on door panels and console.

The standard all-vinyl interior comes in black, saddle, dark brown, dark green, blue and red.

No matter if your mission's only a trip to the drive-in, the interior of the 1970 Corvette is designed to put you in complete control.

Chevrolet Corvette Custom Interior and Tilt-Telescopic steering column.

9

Links: Innenseite aus dem 1970er Corvette-Prospekt. Rechts: Starke Nummer – 425 SAE-PS werden geboten. Vorsorglich wird der Wagen auf einer (leeren) Rennstrecke gezeigt.

Strength in numbers for 1971- 270, 330, 365, 425 hp.

Every Corvette is built tough right from the start. Our basic V8, the 270-hp Turbo-Fire 350, features an 8.5:1 compression ratio, a 4-barrel carb, cast aluminum alloy pistons and a precision-formed crank. With this, and all other Corvette engines, you get Corvette's dual exhausts with rectangular outlets and Positraction differential standard.

Go one step up to the 330-hp Turbo-Fire 350, and you get a 9.0:1 compression ratio, impact-extruded aluminum alloy pistons, finned aluminum rocker covers, a special-performance cam, mechanical lifters and a forged steel-alloy crank. Plus an aluminum intake manifold, high-domed hood, transistor ignition.

Next step up. Our 365-hp 454-cu.-in. Turbo-Jet V8. This engine with 8.5:1 compression ratio uses a dual-snorkel air cleaner with a chromed cover and an extra-large oil pan. You also get a high-domed hood, a larger diameter front stabilizer bar, heavier duty rear wheel spindle support arms, a rear suspension stabilizer bar, a larger capacity radiator, dual pulleys for the fan and water pump and a higher performance starter motor.

Also available: our 425-hp Turbo-Jet 454 with a large 4-barrel carb, high-performance cam, mechanical lifters, 9.0:1 compression ratio and aluminum cylinder heads. Plus chassis items included with the 365-hp V8.

Transmissions: standard gearbox is a floor-mounted, wide-range 4-Speed, 2.52:1 low gear. Also available, a close-ratio version with a 2.20:1 low (close ratio not available with 270-hp engine, wide range not available with 425-hp engine). A Special 4-Speed close ratio box is available with the 425-hp V8.

With the 270-, 365-, and 425-hp engines, you can order Turbo Hydra-matic.

Chevrolet Corvette Stingray Convertible with removable hardtop.

Aufnahmen aus einem '73er Katalog. Interessant, daß man „Stingray" jetzt nicht mehr in zwei Worten schreibt.

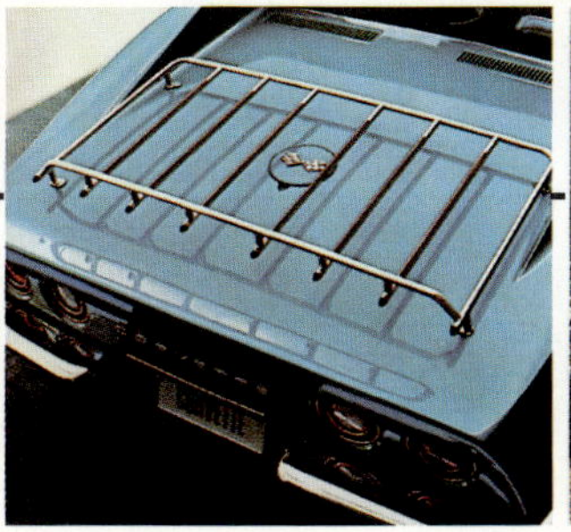

Corvette Stingray Convertible
es being under the weather a
sure. All you have to do with the
ng top is unlatch it, raise it, drop it,
it and forget it. The deck cover
s it all. Top available in both
k and white.

can also order a removable hard-
t's well worth having. For winter,
ariety and for saving your
ng top for a sunny day.

Corvette Instrument Panel is
like a cockpit than a dashboard.
o right: a big speedometer and an
lly big tachometer. The five other
es tell you the coolant temperature,
essure, amperage, fuel level and
ne. Above the gauges on the con-
controls for the windshield washers
wipers. Below, heating and venti-
g controls. Within easy reach is the
FM radio or AM/FM/Stereo radio
an order. With one speaker for
And one for your co-pilot.

The Standard Corvette Interior is up to pretty high standards.
The high-backed contoured bucket seats are virtually handmade. They're cushioned with thick foam and have built-in head restraints. Fold either seat forward and you're into Corvette's fully carpeted, illuminated luggage area. Two storage compartments are concealed behind the seats. A third compartment conceals the battery. The remainder of the passenger area is trimmed in rich padded vinyl with deep twist carpeting on the floor. Available in black, blue, medium saddle, dark saddle and red.

The Available Custom Corvette Interior (shown at left). The seat panels are genuine leather with matching vinyl trim. There are wood-grained vinyl accents on the doors and console. Underfoot, deep cut-pile nylon carpeting. You're literally riding in the lap of luxury. Black, medium saddle or dark saddle.

BUILDING A BETTER WAY TO SEE THE U.S.A.
Chevrolet

OPTIONS

Corvette-Werbung 1974 – einmal ganz anders. Fotos und leichte Aquarelle geben einen ungewöhnlichen Kontrast. In kleingedruckten Zeilen wird darauf hingewiesen, daß man auch Ledersitze haben kann.

FOR THE BODY

Removable Hardtop (for convertible)—The way to give your convertible top a vacation during cold weather. And yourself the added warmth and quiet of a hardtop. It's styled to enhance the lines of the Corvette and can be ordered to match the exterior color, or with an available black vinyl roof cover for a more formal look.

Luggage Rack (dealer-installed)—It's handsome enough to be strictly a dress-up item. But isn't it nice that it also lets you store the occasional overflow from your luggage compartment?

Also Available (from your dealer)— • Right-hand outside mirror • Non-vented locking gas cap.

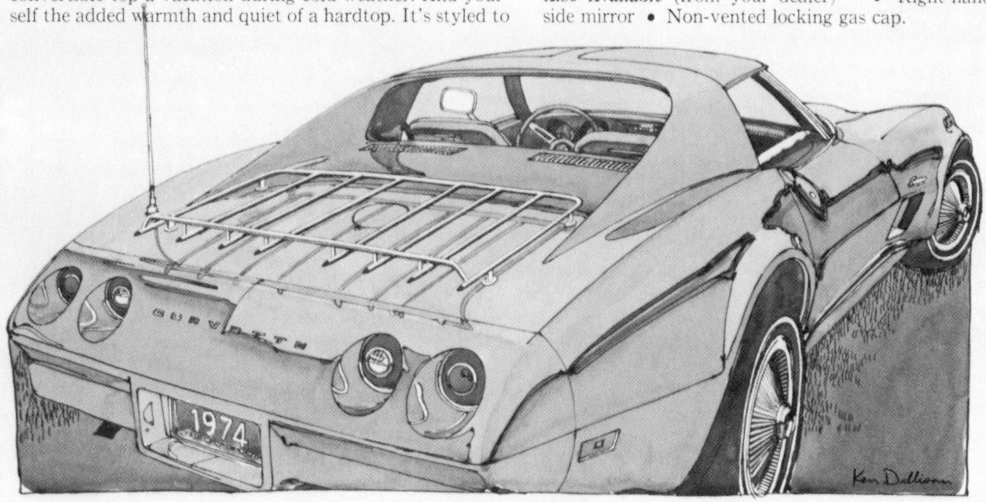

FOR THE CHASSIS

Turbo-Fire 350-4 Special V8—When we say that we've given this 350 a special carb, cam, crank, cylinder heads, pistons, rods, even finned aluminum rocker arm covers, we still haven't said it all. Designed to come on in the higher RPM numbers, the Special is obviously an engine for the enthusiast.

Turbo-Jet 454-4 V8—Like they say: "Nothing beats inches." And with 454 cubic inches of displacement, the Turbo-Jet provides a lusty torque output over the entire RPM operating range. This engine, like all 1974 Corvette engines, features a new multi-louvered radiator for improved cooling in city traffic conditions.

Console-Shift Turbo Hydra-matic Transmission—Think of this automatic three-speed as a box with a dual personality. Leave it in "Drive" range when you've got other things on your mind. Shift it manually with the console T-handle when special acceleration or engine braking needs are called for. Available with all engines.

Close-Ratio 4-Speed Manual Transmission—Fully synchronized with a 2.20:1 first gear ratio, this gearbox provides

Schwarz und stark – und jetzt mit dem beliebten T-Top!

The essence.

This is what makes your Corvette what it is: America's only true production sports car.

ON THE OUTSIDE.

Corvette's low-slung aerodynamic styling and fiberglass body need no introduction. Also:

• Lightweight, remove-and-store roof panels convert your Corvette in seconds from closed- to open-top coupe, or vice versa. This year we've made provisions to stow the panels on the available deck-lid luggage carrier if you wish, to give more interior luggage room (see back cover).
• Energy-absorbing bumpers covered by soft, molded urethane in body color.
• Dual molded bumper guards, front and rear.
• Flush, retracting dual headlamps; dual-unit circular taillights.
• Soft-Ray tinted glass.
• Black windshield posts give new "thin pillar" look.
• 15″ x 8″ steel wheels with bright hub covers and trim rings.
• Hide-A-Way windshield wipers.
• New exterior colors: yellow, black, dark red, orange, dark blue, light blue metallic, tan buckskin. Continued: classic white, silver and medium red.

THE COCKPIT.

It's intimate as only a two-seater can be, yet functional as a sports car must be.

• Two-level instrumentation. Tachometer and speedometer with trip odometer are centered in front of the driver's eyes, high on the panel (just below the driver's road view) on two large circular dials. Voltmeter, coolant temperature, oil pressure, fuel level and electric clock are on a separate panel, in smaller, aircraft-styled dials, at the forward end of the console.
• Center console puts the following controls at your right hand: shift selector (with new leather boot); heating/ventilation plus ashtray and lighter. Controls for available air conditioning, power windows, Electro-Clear rear window defogger with warning light are also located on the console. New features include a handy coin tray and a soft vinyl housing over the parking brake handle.
• Four-spoke, padded-vinyl-covered steering wheel is now positioned two inches farther from driver to ease entry and exit.
• New column-mounted "Smart Switch" puts these controls at your left hand: turn signals, hi-lo headlight beam selection, windshield wipers and washers.
• Padded sun shades now swivel to provide some glare protection from side as well as front.
• Overhead and underpanel courtesy lights actuate automatically when either door opens, or manually with headlight switch.
• Panel-mounted map pockets.
• Extensive sound insulation.
• Nylon, cut-pile, color-keyed carpeting for passenger and luggage compartment.
• Luggage compartment behind seats and two storage chambers (one lockable for valuables), featuring increased ease of access for '77.
• Now standard is custom-level interior trim, featuring choice of leather (back cover) or cloth-and-leather seating surfaces (below) on full foam, deep-contoured bucket seats. Select from black, buckskin, red, smoke gray, blue or brown. Or choose from leather-seat interiors in white with buckskin, red, smoke gray or blue accents.

THE POWER TEAM.

Get the one that best suits your personal driving preferences.

• The standard 350 4-barrel V8 is a rugged power plant with impressive low-speed torque for around-town cruising, but also very willing and responsive on the highway.
• The standard wide-ratio 4-Speed manual transmission is great for normal driving. The high numerical first-gear ratio gets you off the mark smartly, while wide-range intermediate ratios provide good torque matching at low and intermediate speeds.

Engines (5.7 Litre)	Transmissions	Rear Axle Ratios
Standard 350 4-barrel V8 Net HP*, 180 @ 4000 RPM Torque, 270 ft.-lbs. @ 2400 RPM	4-Speed, Wide Ratio, Std.†**	3.36, Std. 3.08, Avail.
	Turbo Hydra-matic, Avail.	3.08, Std.
Available† Special 350 4-barrel V8 Net HP*, 210 @ 5200 RPM Torque, 255 ft.-lbs. @ 3600 RPM	4-Speed, Wide Ratio, Std.†**	3.70, Std. 3.55, Avail.
	4-Speed, Close Ratio, Avail.†**	3.70, Std. 3.55, Avail.
	Turbo Hydra-matic, Avail.	3.55, Std.

SPECIAL NOTE: California Emission Equipment required for registration in California. In other states, High Altitude Emission Equipment may be required in areas 4,000 or more feet above sea level.
*SAE net (as installed) rating.
†Not available in California.
**High Altitude Emission Equipment.

CORVETTE ENGINES HAVE:

• High Energy Ignition, a solid-state system that delivers up to 85% hotter spark to the plugs than a conventional system.
• Hydraulic valve lifters.
• Coolant recovery system to help reduce coolant loss.
• Delcotron generator with solid-state regulator.
• Freedom battery needs no refills. Side terminals eliminate corrosion buildup. 3,500-watt rating.
• Long recommended maintenance intervals: Spark plugs, up to 22,500 miles; engine oil, 6 months or 7,500 miles; oil filter, first 7,500 miles, then every 15,000 miles; chassis lube, 6 months or 7,500 miles; automatic transmission fluid, 60,000 miles. Check details in the Owner's Manual.

FOR SAFETY AND SECURITY.

Occupant protection.
• Two combination seat and inertia reel shoulder belts for driver (with reminder light and buzzer) and right seat passenger.
• Energy-absorbing steering column.
• Safety steering wheel.
• Passenger-guard door locks.
• Safety door latches and hinges
• Folding seat back latches.
• Energy-absorbing padded i strument panel.
• Thick-laminate windshield.
• Safety armrests.

Accident prevention.
• Side marker lights an flectors.
• Parking lamps that illu with headlamps.
• Four-way hazard warn flasher.
• Lane-change feature in direction signal control.
• Backup lights.
• Windshield defrosters, washers and dual-speed wipers.
• Wide-view inside day-night mirror (vinyl-edged, shatter-resistant glass and deflecting support).
• Outside rearview mirror.
• Dual master cylinder brake system with warning light.
• Starter safety switch.

Anti-theft.
• Alarm set or deactivated by key lock in left front fender.
• Ignition-key reminder buzzer.
• Steering column lock.

• Head room: 36.2″.
Shoulder room: 47.9″.
Hip room: 48.8″.
Leg room: 52.1″.
Luggage space:
7.8 cu.ft.

• Power steering.

• Magic-Mirror acrylic exterior finish.

• Fully independent front and rear suspension.

• Fiberglass body construction can't rust or corrode.

• Wide 15″x8″ wheels.
Wheelbase: 98.0″.
Overall length: 185.2″.
Overall width: 69.0″.
Loaded height: 48.0″.
Tread: front—58.7″, rear—59.5″.

• Fuel tank rated capacity: 18 gals.

• New stainless steel covers on mufflers —added protection against corrosion.

• Power disc brakes at all four wheels. Fade-resistant and self-adjusting.

• Protective fiberglass inner fenders, front and rear.

• Corvette-specification, GR70-series, steel-belted radial ply tires.

Unübersehbar der Hinweis, daß die Corvette nach Kalifornien in modifizierter Ausführung geliefert wird. Aber mit Pferdestärken wird nach wie vor nicht gegeizt.

Chevrolet
CORVETTE
25
1953 ANNIVERSARY 1978

Links: Ende 1977 erschien dieses Faltblatt mit der 25jährigen Geschichte der Corvette. Rechts die Spezifikation des aktuellen Wagens.

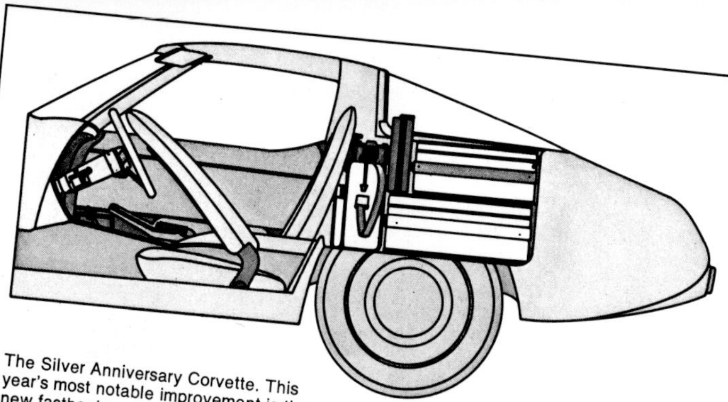

The Silver Anniversary Corvette. This year's most notable improvement is the new fastback roofline and rear window which enhance Corvette's sleek silhouette. Additionally, the new rear window not only allows for a cleaner styling profile, it also improves driver visibility and adds luggage space. There's a roll shade to screen the luggage space. And there's room inside for storage of removable roof panels.

Also new for 1978 is a larger, plastic-lined fuel tank. Capacity has been boosted from 17 to 24 gallons.

The instrument panel has also been restyled and features face-mounted, round instruments which are extremely legible as well as handsome. A new glove box has been added, too.

Corvette performance has been improved with a dual snorkel air cleaner and new low-restriction exhaust system and mufflers on the available L82 350 Cu. In. V8 engine (not available in California). The transverse rear leaf spring in the independent rear suspension has been widened to reduce stress.

Two new transmissions are introduced in 1978. A new Four-Speed manual transmission is standard. A new automatic transmission is available for the L82 350 Cu. In. V8 engine. And in recognition of Corvette's 25th year, Silver Anniversary emblems are mounted on the nose and rear deck.

Corvette continues to offer a long list of standard equipment:

- 4-barrel 350 Cu. In. V8.
- Choice of 4-Speed manual or automatic transmission.
- Independent suspension, front and rear.
- Power steering.
- Reinforced fiberglass body construction that can't rust or corrode.
- Power disc brakes at all four wheels; self-adjusting and fade-resistant.
- Low-profile, steel-belted radial ply tires.
- Wide 15″ x 8″ wheels.
- Body-colored, energy-absorbing bumpers.
- Flush-mounted, retractable headlights.
- Soft-Ray tinted glass.
- Center console.
- Column-mounted switch that controls turn signals, high and low headlight beams.
- Choice of leather or cloth and leather seat inserts.
- Full foam, deep contoured bucket seats.
- Choice of 10 exterior colors, 7 interior colors.
- Carpeted floor, including tunnel sides and door sills.
- Twin bumper guards, front and rear.
- Removable roof panels.
- Automatic overhead and instrument panel courtesy lights.
- Extensive sound insulation.
- Electric clock.
- Lockable storage compartments.
- Full instrumentation, including speedometer, tachometer, water temperature gage, fuel gage, voltmeter, oil pressure gage, and trip odometer.
- Delco Freedom battery that needs no water.
- High Energy Ignition system.
- Delcotron generator with solid-state voltage regulator.
- Fiberglass inner fenders.

Long recommended service intervals under normal driving conditions.

Engine oil	12 months or 7,500 miles
Chassis lubrication	12 months or 7,500 miles
Oil filter	First 7,500 miles. Every 15,000 miles thereafter.
Spark plugs	Up to 22,500 miles
Automatic transmission fluid	60,000 miles

SAFETY FEATURES

OCCUPANT PROTECTION FEATURES • Continuous loop seat belt and inertia reel shoulder harness for driver (with reminder light and buzzer) and passenger • Padded sun visors • Energy-absorbing steering column • Passenger guard door locks • Safety door latches and stamped steel hinges • Folding seat-back latches • Energy-absorbing padded instrument panel and front seat-back tops • Thick laminate windshield • Safety armrests • Safety steering wheel.

ACCIDENT PREVENTION FEATURES • Side marker lights and reflectors • Parking lamps that illuminate with headlamps • Four-way hazard warning flasher • Back-up lights • Lane change feature in direction signal control • Windshield defrosters, washer and dual-speed wipers • Wide-view inside mirror (vinyl-edged, shatter-resistant glass and deflecting support) • Outside rearview mirror • Dual master cylinder brake system with warning light • Starter safety switch.

ANTI-THEFT FEATURES • Anti-theft ignition key reminder buzzer • Anti-theft steering column lock • Anti-theft alarm system with concealed exterior switch, including (for the first time) the roof panels in its circuitry.

ENGINE AVAILABILITY

All states except California		**Transmissions/Rear Axle Ratios**			
				Automatic Transmission	
Engines	**Power Rating†**	**4-Speed Manual**	**4-Speed Close-Ratio Manual**	**Below 4,000 Ft.**	**4,000 Ft. and Above**
350 Cu. In. V8 (Std.)	185/175▲	3.36	NA	3.08	3.55
350 Cu. In. V8 (Avail. RPO L82)•	220	3.70/3.36*	3.70	3.55	NA
California only					
350 Cu. In. V8	175	NA	NA	3.55	NA

*†S.A.E. net horsepower as installed. *Available highway ratio. STD.—Standard. NA—Not available. ▲Rating with High Altitude Emission Equipment.*
•Not available California, Maryland, Florida, Oregon, Washington, also Boston, Chicago, Des Plaines (Ill.), Barrington (Ill.), Grand Rapids (Mi.) and Cook County (Ill.).
SPECIAL NOTE: California Emission Equipment required for registration in California. In other states, High Altitude Emission Equipment may be required in areas 4,000 feet or more above sea level.

The 25th Anniversary Corvette.

It stands alone today as it has since the summer of 1953, a truly unique and finely machined two-seater, America's only true production sports car.

The legend lives on and improves, as legends do, with the passage of time.

The Silver Anniversary Corvette: Twenty-five years in the making, and we've enjoyed every minute of it.

And now, if you will, a round of applause for the Corvette founding fath Harley Earl, Zora Arkus-Duntov, Bill Mitchell, Ed Cole…

Available on any Corvette are many Options and Custom Features. Many are illustrated or described in this catalog. Availability often depends on the model and other equipment selected. Your Chevrole

Der Faltprospekt (Seite 60/61) ließ sich zum Poster ausklappen und enthält auf der Rückseite diese dreifache Dame mit ihrem silberfarbenen Traumwagen Modell 1978. Unten die Titelseite eines 1979er Faltprospektes, der ebenfalls eine Überraschung enthielt – ein gezeichnetes Poster (siehe Seite 64).

corvette

The only true American production sports car. An automotive classic that's become a legend among those who know and love fine automobiles. Classic in line, in detail, in capability and in innovative engineering, Corvette has a look, a feel, a way of moving that sets it apart.
Corvette. The pride of Chevrolet. The one and only.

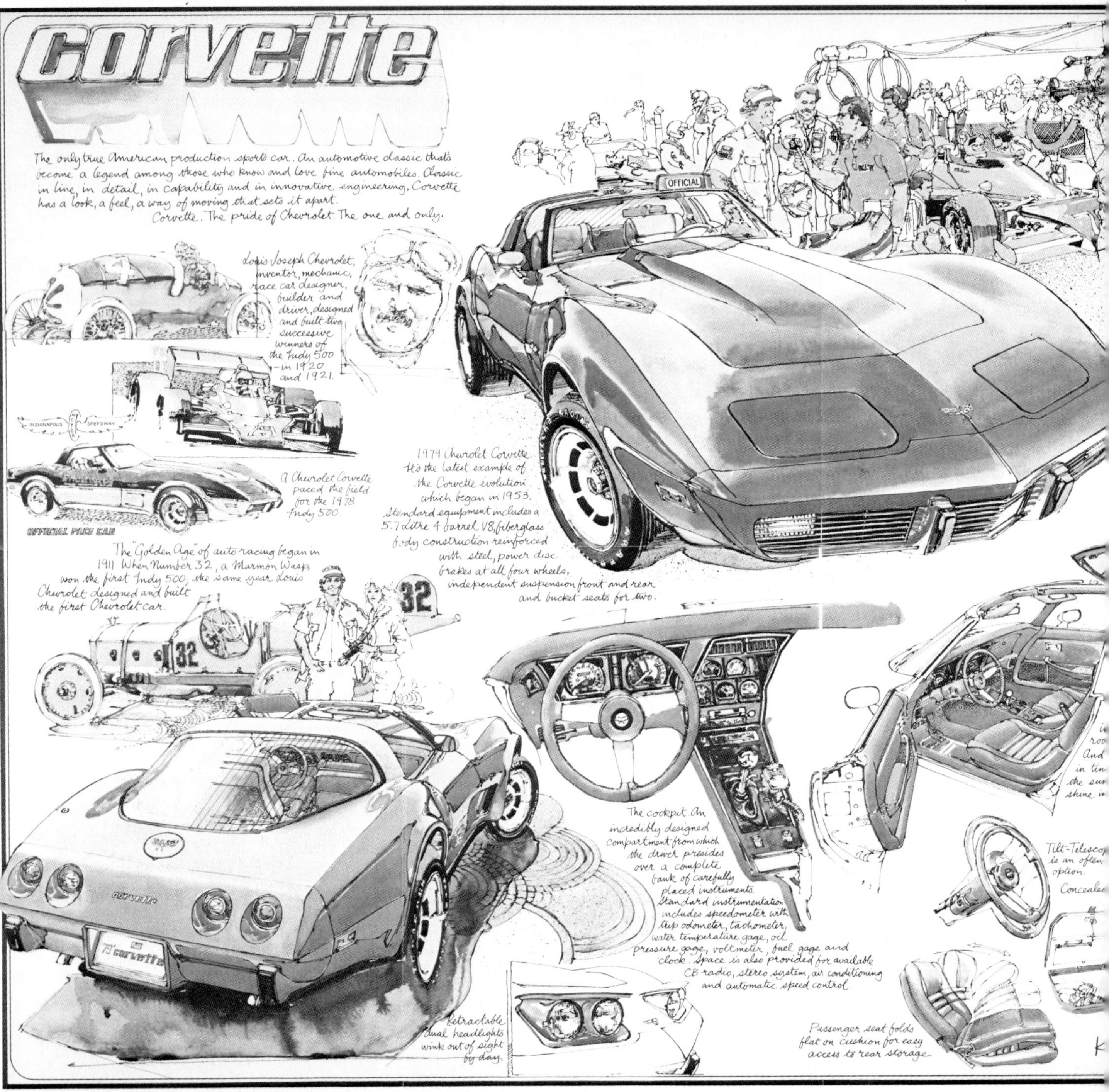

Louis Joseph Chevrolet, inventor, mechanic, race car designer, builder and driver, designed and built two successive winners of the Indy 500 — in 1920 and 1921.

A Chevrolet Corvette paced the field for the 1978 Indy 500.

1979 Chevrolet Corvette. It's the latest example of the Corvette evolution which began in 1953. Standard equipment includes a 5.7 Litre 4 barrel V8, fiberglass body construction reinforced with steel, power disc brakes at all four wheels, independent suspension front and rear and bucket seats for two.

The "Golden Age" of auto racing began in 1911 when Number 32, a Marmon Wasp, won the first Indy 500, the same year Louis Chevrolet designed and built the first Chevrolet car.

The cockpit. An incredibly designed compartment from which the driver presides over a complete bank of carefully placed instruments. Standard instrumentation includes speedometer with trip odometer, tachometer, water temperature gage, oil pressure gage, voltmeter, fuel gage and clock. Space is also provided for available CB radio, stereo system, air conditioning and automatic speed control.

Retractable dual headlights wink out of sight by day.

Passenger seat folds flat on cushion for easy access to rear storage.

i
roo
And
in tin
the su
shine i

Tilt-Telesco
is an often
option.
Concealed

K

Die Zusammenstellung diverser Extras zu einem „persönlichen" Wagen ließ die GM-Texter zur Aussage verleiten: Bauen Sie sich Ihre eigene Corvette!

Build your own Corvette.

(See your dealer for current ordering information and specific model/option availability.)

COLORS

Exterior color ______

Interior color† ______

Upholstery ______

ENGINES

(See Power Teams chart for details on engine and transmission availability.)

☐ 5.7 Litre 4-Bbl. V8 (350 Cu. In.) (Std.)

☐ 5.7 Litre 4-Bbl. V8 (350 Cu. In.) L82 (Avail.)*

TRANSMISSIONS

☐ Four-Speed manual*

☐ Four-Speed manual close-ratio*

☐ Automatic

AVAILABLE OPTIONS

☐ Air conditioning.

☐ Removable tinted glass roof panels.

☐ Tilt-Telescopic steering wheel.

☐ Automatic speed control.

☐ Electric rear window defogger.

☐ Power windows.

☐ Power windows and door locks.

☐ Sport mirrors, LH remote and RH manual.

☐ Convenience Group (includes time-delay dome and courtesy lights, headlight warning buzzer, underhood light, low fuel warning light, color-keyed floor mats, intermittent windshield wipers and RH visor vanity mirror).

SOUND EQUIPMENT

☐ AM/FM stereo/Citizens Band radio with tri-band power antenna.

☐ AM/FM stereo radio.

☐ AM/FM stereo radio with 8-track stereo tape.

☐ AM/FM stereo radio with stereo cassette tape.

☐ Power antenna.

☐ Dual rear speakers.

TIRES

☐ P225/70R-15 steel-belted radial ply white-lettered tires.

☐ P255/60R-15 aramid-belted radial ply white-lettered tires.

MISCELLANEOUS

☐ Aluminum wheels.

☐ Gymkhana suspension.

☐ Chassis equipment — trailering.

☐ Heavy-duty battery.

☐ Highway axle ratio.

☐ Heavy-duty shock absorbers.

*Not available in California or with High Altitude Emission Equipment.

† Leather or cloth and leather interior colors available: light beige, dark blue, dark green, oyster. Leather only: black, red.

A word about assembly, components and optional equipment in these Chevrolets.

The Chevrolets described in this brochure are assembled at facilities of General Motors Corporation operated by the GM Assembly Division. These vehicles incorporate thousands of different components produced by various divisions of General Motors and by various suppliers to General Motors. From time to time during the manufacturing process, it may be necessary, in order to meet public demand for particular vehicles or equipment, or to meet federally mandated emissions, safety and fuel economy requirements, or for other reasons, to produce Chevrolet products with different components or differently sourced components than initially scheduled. All such components have been approved for use in Chevrolet products and will provide the quality performance associated with the Chevrolet name.

With respect to extra cost optional equipment, make certain you specify the type of equipment you desire on your vehicle when ordering it from your dealer. Some options may be unavailable when your car is built. Your dealer receives advice regarding current availability of options. You may ask the dealer for this information. GM also requests the dealer to advise you if an option you ordered is unavailable. We suggest you verify that your car includes the optional equipment you ordered or, if there are changes, that they are acceptable to you.

Seiten aus einem 198 Corvette-Prospekt.

Corvette is a rolling showcase of new technology, new materials and new thinking—all part of an evolutionary process that continues year after year. Adherence to the principle of engineering excellence has been applied to all areas, from the front bumpers to the aircraft-style cockpit to the rear suspension system. It is these kinds of developments—detailed here—that make Corvette what it is today: one of the most renowned two-seat sports cars in the world.

For 1981, Corvette engineers trod where none have gone before by developing the world's first and only fiberglass-reinforced composite automotive spring (used with automatic transmission only). It even won the Society of Plastic Engineers Grand Award. This monoleaf rear spring—at 8 lbs.—replaces a 41-lb. steel multileaf spring. And it's not just lighter, it's more efficient. It can store six times the strain-energy per unit weight than a comparable weight of spring steel. This is the lightest possible leaf spring application to be found in any automotive suspension. And steel interleaf friction is eliminated. This fiberglass spring supports the weight of the car that rests on the rear wheels and provides suspension compliance. Wheel position is controlled by a system of links and pivots.

Attention to detail for 1981 includes other engineering developments such as magnesium valve rocker covers and stainless steel exhaust manifolds. And an

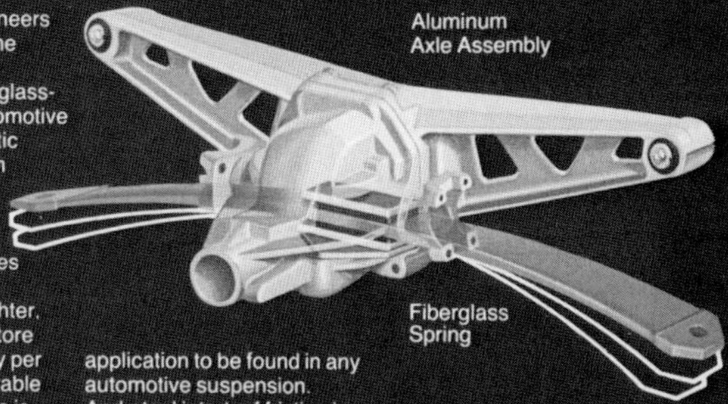

"We critique Corvette with the same engineering objectivity we'd use to evaluate a military aircraft: What is Corvette's mission? How well does it carry out that mission?"

Dave McLellan,
Chief Engineer, Corvette

1982 CORVETTE
Chevy makes good things happen.
corvette
Chevrolet
ette Coupe.

1982 Corvette

This is a whole new kind of Corvette.

It is still the road-rapacious sports car that's always been capable of inhaling great chunks of tormented 2-lane tarmac and leaving you exhilarated even after long, 1000-mile days in the saddle. It's still the time and space machine it's always been.

But there's a new civility now, predicated in large part on two engineering advances for 1982. Cross-fire fuel injection and a 4-speed automatic transmission with overdrive fourth gear so good in every aspect of driving usage that the manual transmission has been deleted.

There's a new quality about Corvette too. A space age standard of fit and finish quality that is rigidly imposed and then double-checked by workers and inspectors at Corvette's new 1-million-square-foot plant in Bowling Green, Kentucky.

And for this year, a unique and distinguished Corvette . . . the special "Collector Edition".

This is the Corvette to covet. From its raised white-lettered Eagle GT tires to its frameless hatchback, the "Collector Edition" is, we believe, the finest all-around 2-seater in the world.

Corvette Coupe.

Frameless glass-hatch design with remote release is standard on the "Collector Edition" Hatchback Coupe.

Aircraft-style centre console and full gauge instrumentation are standard.
NOTE: Speedometers in Canada have major scale in km/h, secondary in mph and odometer in kilometres.

Corvette standard interior.

Einfach in Druck und Gestaltung ist dieser Prospekt. Aber er zeigt alle Einzelheiten.

Corvette Major Standard Equipment

EXTERIOR	Corvette Sport Coupe	Corvette Collector Edition
Anti-theft alarm system with starter-interrupt feature	S	S
Front fender louvres	S	S
Front cornering lamps	S	S
Specific "Collector Edition" emblems – front, sides, rear	NA	S
Power-operated retractable headlamps	S	S
Quad headlamps with halogen hi-beam inner units	S	S
Dual remote-controlled outside sport mirrors	S	S
Tinted glass	S	S
Special silver-beige metallic finish	NA	S
Removable roof panels with solar screening	EC	S
Steel wheels with centre hub and trim rings	S	NA
Finned aluminum wheels	NA	S
Frameless rear hatch glass with remote release	NA	S
Body-colour front bumper with integral air dam	S	S
Energy-absorbing bumper systems	S	S
Corrosion-resistant steel-reinforced fiberglass body	S	S
Concealed dual-speed wipers with integral washers and wiper arms	S	S
INTERIOR		
Leather-trimmed vinyl or all-cloth bucket seats	S	NA
Full-leather bucket seats	NA	S
Soft-padded and carpeted door panels	S	S
Moulded shell seats with high-pivot folding backs	S	S
Power windows	S	S
Electric rear window defroster	S	S
AM/FM push-button radio with dual front speakers and mast antenna	S	S
Air conditioning	S	S
Time-delay dome and courtesy lights	S	S
Headlamp-on reminder	S	S
Low-fuel warning lamp	S	S
Illuminated RH visor vanity mirror	S	S
Leather-wrapped steering wheel rim	S	S
Tilt-Telescopic steering wheel and column	S	S
Glove compartment lock and lamp	S	S
Intermittent windshield wipers	S	S
7,000-RPM electronic tachometer	S	S
Voltmeter, temperature, fuel and oil pressure gauges	S	S
Quartz analog electric clock with sweep-second hand	S	S

	Corvette Sport Coupe	Corvette Collector Edition
Cigarette lighter and ashtray	S	S
Resettable trip odometer	S	S
Centre console with shifter, coin tray, window, mirror and air conditioning controls	S	S
Day/night rearview mirror	S	S
Deep-twist floor and stowage area carpet	S	S
Acoustical insulation package	S	S
Luggage compartment concealment shade	S	S
POWER TEAMS/CHASSIS/MECHANICAL		
Computer Command Control	S	S
5.7 Litre CFI V8 engine (Cross-Fire Injection)	S	S
Automatic transmission with overdrive fourth gear	S	S
Aluminum intake manifold with tuned runners	S	S
Stainless steel exhaust manifolds and free-flow mufflers	S	S
Hydraulic valve lifters and exhaust valve rotators	S	S
Magnesium valve rocker covers	S	S
Black wrinkle-finish air cleaner	S	S
Hood outside-air duct	S	S
Electric in-tank fuel pump	S	S
Low-drag engine primary cooling fan	S	S
Auxiliary electric engine cooling fan	S	S
High Energy Ignition system	S	S
Freedom II battery with sealed side terminals	S	S
Power steering with ball-race gear	S	S
Power disc brakes at all four wheels	S	S
Exclusive monoleaf fiberglass rear spring design	S	S
New driveshaft seals and splash shields	S	S
New, larger drive shaft universal joints	S	S
Sturdy frame structure with corrosion-resistant coating	S	S
Fully independent four-wheel suspension	S	S
Delcotron generator with built-in solid-state regulator	S	S
P225/70R-15B steel-belted radial ply tires	S	NA
P225/60R-15B steel-belted radial ply white-lettered tires	EC	S
Compact spare tire	S	S
Side-lift jack	S	S
Underhood lamp	S	S

S-Standard EC-Optional at Extra Cost NA-Not Available

Options

Listed below are some of the available equipment choices to help you customize your 1982 Corvette. For other optional equipment and their availability, see your Chevrolet dealer.

• Electric twin remote control sport mirrors • Roof panel carrier • Power door lock system • Delco radios: AM/FM stereo radio • Electronically tuned stereo radio with 8-track tape player • Electronically tuned stereo radio with cassette tape player • Electronically tuned stereo radio with Citizens Band and cassette tape • Power antenna (included with Citizens Band radio) • Removable glass roof panels • Automatic speed control with 'resume speed' feature • Gymkhana suspension includes rear stabilizer and bushings, higher-rate springs and special shock absorbers • Tires: P225/70R-15 or P225/60R-15 steel-belted radial ply white-lettered • Six-way power driver's seat • Aluminum wheels • Custom two-tone exterior paint.

Exterior Colours

Choose from 11 high-lustre acrylic finishes or several available Two-Tone combinations. Colours: White, Silver Metallic, Black, Silver Blue Metallic, Dark Blue Metallic, Silver Green Metallic, Bright Blue Metallic, Gold Metallic, Charcoal Metallic, Red, Dark Claret Metallic.

Corvette "Collector Edition" features an exclusive Silver Beige Metallic exterior finish.

Interiors

Corvette is available in a choice of four cloth interiors: Silver Gray, Dark Blue, Camel and Dark Red; or select from six available leather trims: Silver Gray, Charcoal, Dark Blue, Green, Camel or Dark Red.

Corvette "Collector Edition": features full leather seats in an exclusive Silver Beige multi-tone trim.

Safety Features

OCCUPANT PROTECTION
Manual lap/shoulder belts with push-button buckles for driver and right front passenger (driver's side includes visual and audible warning system) • Energy-absorbing steering column • Passenger guard door locks • Safety door latches and stamped steel hinges • Folding seat back latches • Energy-absorbing padded instrument panel with anti-reflective upper surface • Laminated windshield/tempered side and rear glass • Safety armrests • Identification symbols for controls and displays.

ACCIDENT AVOIDANCE
Side marker lights and reflectors • Parking lamps that illuminate with headlamps • Four-way hazard warning flasher • Backup lights • Lane change feature in direction signal control • Windshield defrosters, washer and dual-speed wipers with time-delay feature • Vinyl-edged inside mirror • Dual outside rearview mirrors • Dual master cylinder brake system with warning light • Starter safety switch.

ANTI-THEFT
Audible anti-theft ignition key reminder • Anti-theft steering column lock • Anti-theft audio alarm system with starter-interrupt feature • Inside hood release.

A word about assembly, components and optional equipment in these vehicles.

The vehicles described in this brochure are assembled at various Divisions of General Motors Corporation. These vehicles incorporate thousands of different components produced by General Motors of Canada Limited and related companies and their suppliers. From time to time during the manufacturing process, it may be necessary, in order to meet public demand for particular vehicles or equipment, or to meet federally mandated emission and safety requirements or fuel economy guidelines, or for other reasons, to produce vehicles with different components or differently sourced components than initially scheduled. All such components have been approved for use in our products by General Motors of Canada Limited or related companies and will provide the quality performance associated with our name.

Please note that certain optional equipment can be ordered only in conjunction with other optional equipment. Also, upgrading from specified standard equipment may be necessary when certain optional equipment is ordered. Ask your sales representative for details.

With respect to extra cost optional equipment, make certain you specify the type of equipment you desire on your vehicle when ordering it from your dealer. Some options may be unavailable when your car is built. Your dealer receives advice regarding current availability of options. You may ask the dealer for this information. GM also requests the dealer to advise you if an option you ordered is unavailable. We suggest you verify that your car includes the optional equipment you ordered or, if there are changes, that they are acceptable to you.

All illustrations and specifications contained in this catalogue are based on the latest product information available at time of publication approval. The right is reserved to make changes at any time, without notice, in prices, colours, materials, equipment, specifications and models, and to discontinue models. Some of the equipment shown or described throughout this catalogue is available at extra cost. Check with your Chevrolet dealer for complete information.

General Motors of Canada Limited
Oshawa, Ontario

Printed in Canada November 1981

Technische Einzelheiten der Corvette Jahrgang 1982. Auf die „Collector Edition" wird ausführlich eingegangen.

Multi-tone full leather seats highlight the "Collector Edition" special interior.

Corvette Collector Edition Hatchback Coupe.

Exterior Dimensions: Millimetres (Inches)

Wheelbase	2489 (98.0)
Length (overall)	4707 (185.3)
Width (overall)	1753 (69.0)
Height (loaded)	1219 (48.0)
Tread – front	1491 (58.7)
Tread – rear	1511 (59.5)
Fuel tank capacity: Litres (gals)	90.8 (20)

Interior Dimensions: Millimetres (Inches)

Head room – front	919 (36.2)
Leg room – front	1069 (42.1)
Hip room – front	1267 (49.9)
Shoulder room – front	1206 (47.5)
Usable trunk capacity: Litres (cu. ft.)	234 (8.4)

Corvette Power Teams

Engine	Ordering Code	Displacement (cu. in.)	Engine Availability	Transmission Availability
5.7 Litre Cross-fire Injection V8(A)	L83	350	Std.	Std. 4-speed automatic with overdrive

Std. = Standard (A) = Produced by GM – Chevrolet Motor Division, U.S.A.
Computer Command Control System (NB1) standard.
Caution: The use of leaded fuel will cause the Computer Command Control System to malfunction.

See your Chevrolet salesperson for Transport Canada approved fuel consumption estimates for all Corvette models.

A WORD ABOUT ENGINES

Some Chevrolets are equipped with engines produced by other GM division, subsidiaries, or affiliated companies worldwide. See your dealer for details.

Exportorientiert: Angaben in metrischen Maßen! Das Motorenangebot hat sich drastisch verringert . . .

COMMITMENT

The fact that the first chapter in this Corvette brochure concerns the final chapter in the Corvette building process is in itself significant. We are committed to excellence in the production of the product, in order to achieve excellence in the product.

A good example of the totality of the Corvette commitment is the scene pictured here—"The Morning Audit." Each morning, salaried and hourly employes me examine cars in detail ar search for ways to assur enhance the quality of Co

It is typical of the atten detail in evidence throug the new Corvette plant ir

The Corvette plant, Bowling Green, Kentucky.

10

Eine neue Generation: Corvette-Katalog für den Modelljahrgang 1983.

Alles neu – macht GM **1983**

In gänzlich neuer Aufmachung zeigte sich die Corvette im Modell-Jahrgang 1983. Geblieben war lediglich das V8-Injection-Aggregat mit 350 SAE-PS. Von seinem ursprünglichen „Biß" hatte diese Corvette viel verloren, doch inzwischen war eine neue Automobil-Generation herangewachsen, die ganz andere Maßstäbe anlegte . . .

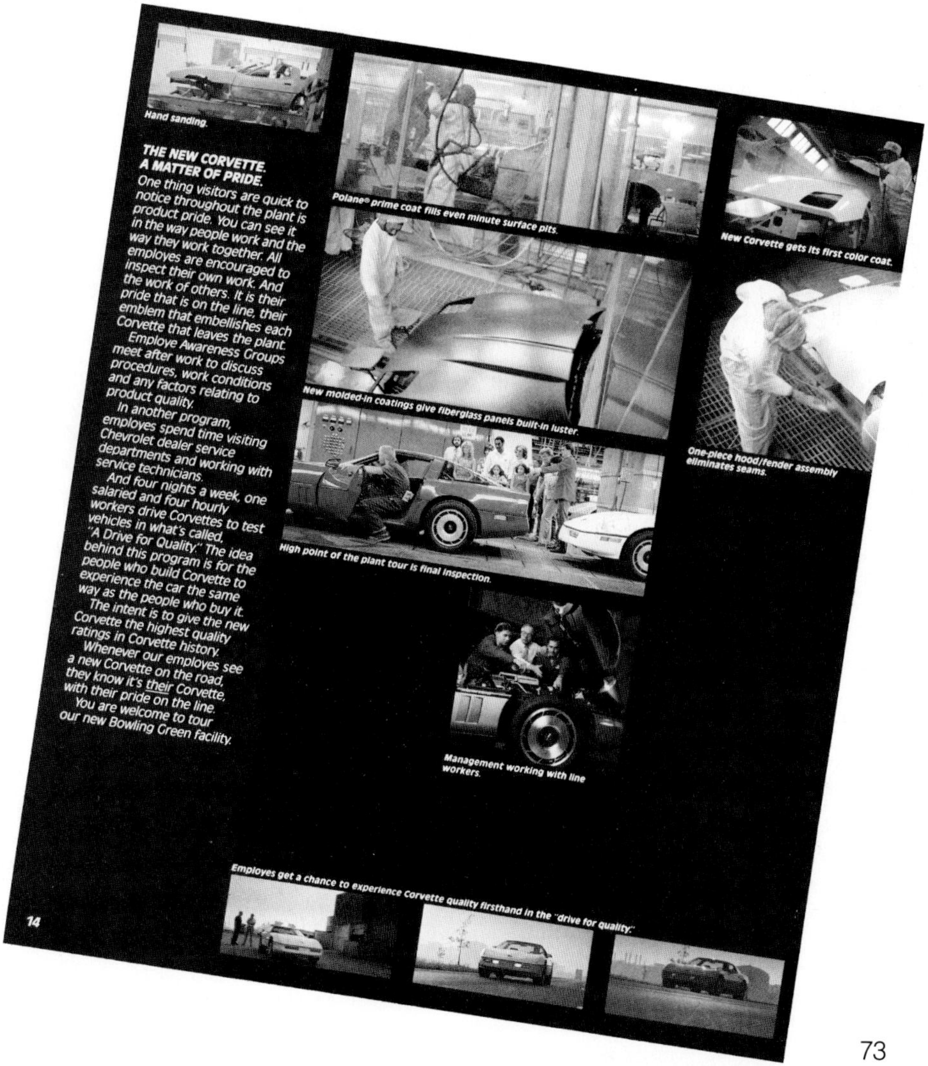

You'd expect the new Corvette to brake handily and it does. With a Girlock four-wheel disc brake system, the new Corvette can decelerate from its top speed as high as 1.0g. Girlock is internationally respected for high performance and racing brake expertise. The low-drag, aluminum caliper design for the new Corvette effects a considerable weight savings over previous Corvette four-wheel disc systems, which helps to reduce unsprung mass. The resulting vehicle dynamics are impressive.

With the standard suspension and the optional Goodyear Eagle VR tires, lateral acceleration is rated at 0.9g on our skidpad, in the hands of a professional driver.

1.0g is equal to the pull of gravity. Cornering or braking at 1.0g means we are encountering a horizontal component (or force) equal in pull to the gravity vector (or the full weight of the car). With Corvette's 0.9g reading, the lateral force is equal to 90% of the weight of the car.

There is an optional suspension, the Z51 Performance Handling Package. It generates 0.95g under lateral acceleration on GM's skidpad. Readings in this range are remarkable, yet Corvette is still a com… able car to drive.

The Z51 incorporates … 9½" rear wheels, larger stabilizer bars, 25mm fro… 23mm rear. Different bus… are used, allowing low defle… while cornering. There ar…

36

Man gibt sich wieder aggressiv – und sei es durch ungewöhnliche Fotowinkel – aber auch ausführlich im Detail.

of the proven and efficient racing engineering practices. The use of forged aluminum suspension components reduced unsprung mass by nearly 30%, which contributes to wheel control, ride and road holding. The payoff is that the new Corvette has demonstrated remarkable directional stability and transient response in surface testing on the GM proving grounds.

The new Corvette. A true world-class sports car.

ences, too, in the stiffness
e fiberglass monoleaf
gs at both front and rear
 the valving of the shocks.
 3.0:1 ratio, power-assisted
and-pinion steering of
51 package makes for
 response to driver control

e suspension of the new
ette is a totally integrated
age which reflects many

37

Inzwischen wurde der Targa-Bügel zum Styling-Element.

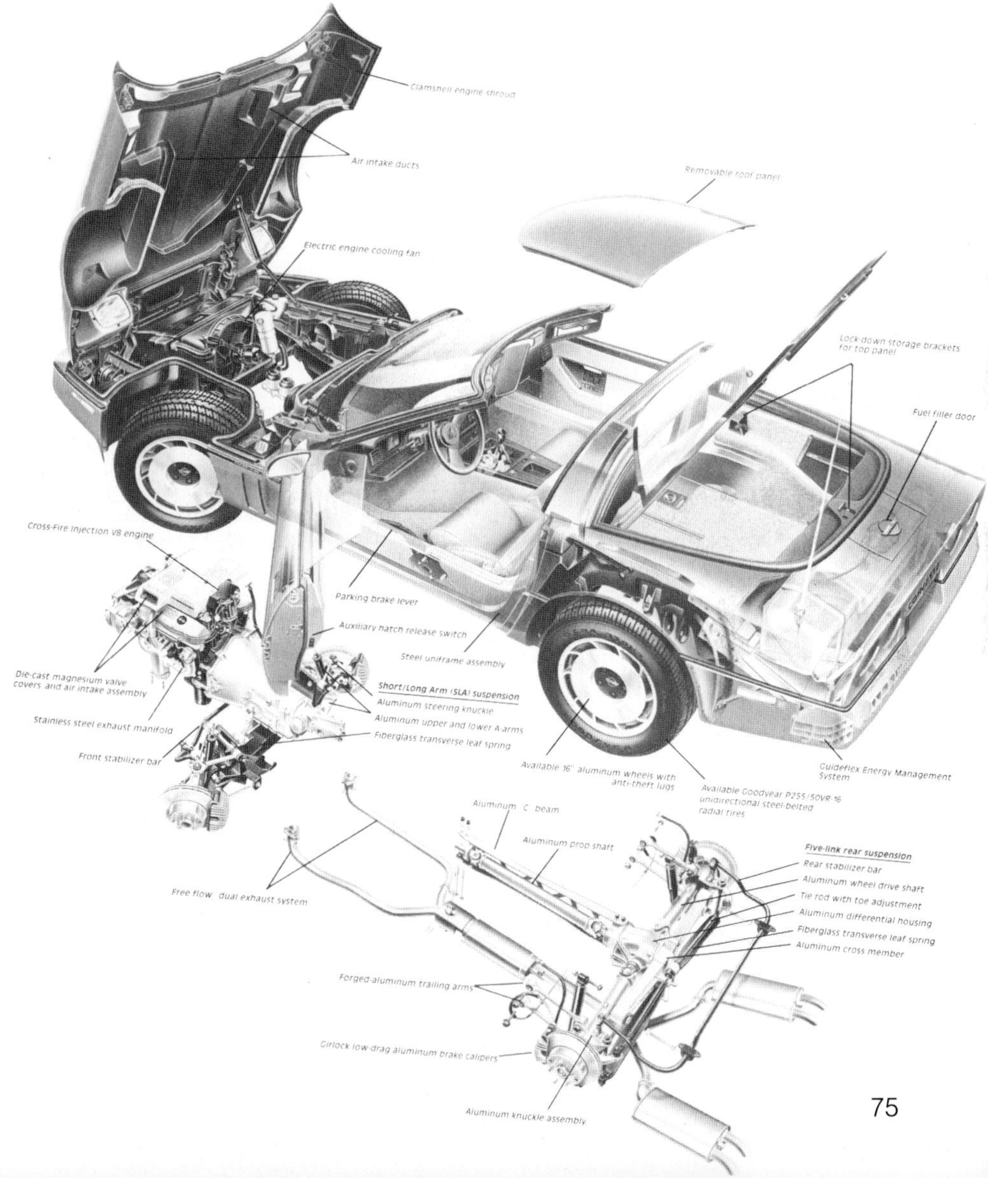

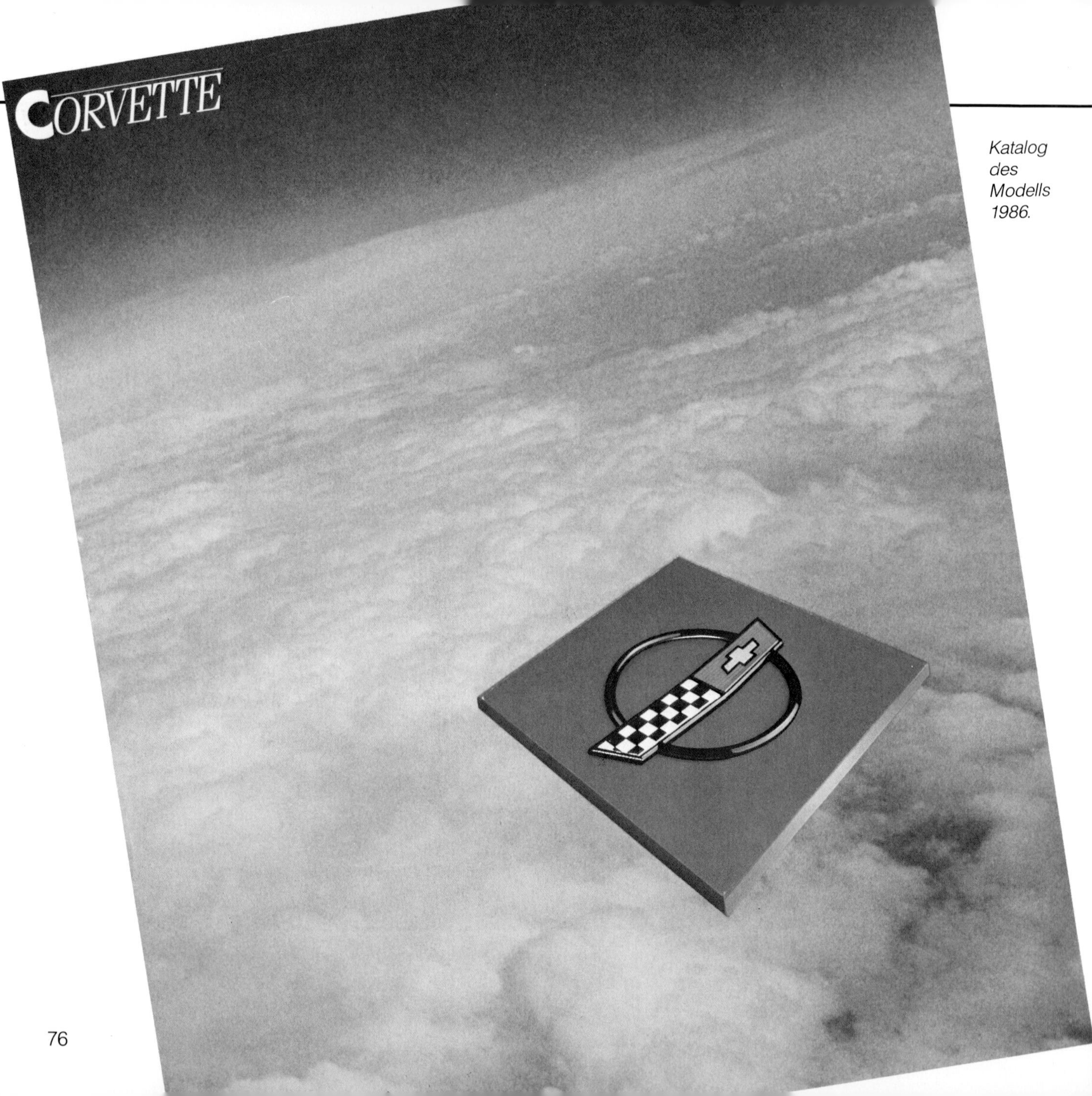

Katalog des Modells 1986.

CARSON WELLS
HOTEL

Der schönste Corvette-Katalog, den es je gab – mit 44 Seiten Inhalt und eingelegten Datenblättern. Auch die Fotos sind von ausgezeichneter Qualität.

NEEDLES, SOUTH DAKOTA. NAMED FOR THE SHARP PEAKS THAT JUT UP FROM THE GRASSES OF THE GREAT PLAINS. HOME OF PRAIRIE DOGS AND BISON; HOST, BRIEFLY, TO CORVETTE.

AMERICA THE VAST, WHERE ROADS THAT STRETCH STRAIGHT TO THE HORIZON ARE AN IDEAL AND INVITING PROVING GROUND FOR THE POWER THAT PULSES THROUGH CORVETTE.

You'd think the sky is the sky everywhere. But people who've grown up under unbroken western vistas feel hemmed in when they travel eastward. And those who like their sky in bits and pieces gaze 360°, shiver a little and say, "There's too much sky," when they go out West.

In the Corvette Convertible you do more than travel under the sky. You become part of it. With nothing between you and the changing face of America… the pungence of freshly turned farmland… the wind blowing from Idaho to Indiana… the Rockies thrust up along the spine of the continent …deserts spread over endless arid miles.

Before long the car assumes the aura of its occupant. Temperature and airflow set to particular preferences. Favorite traveling music modulated precisely. A sweater tossed aside.

When you climb aboard after a brief rest stop, you simply assume everything will be as you left it. After all, you and the Corvette form a private world.

Private but never anonymous. Not in this car. From urban streetside to rural truck stop to western national park, the roadster draws a crowd. Murmurs of approval follow. Children dash excitedly from nose to spoiler as young couples grip hands and promise each other, "Someday." Everybody recognizes the Convertible. Most want to touch it as if a piece of The Dream might rub off. And as the machine speeds into the distance, admiration for its beauty mixes with the wish to be going anywhere in the envious glances of those left behind.

Maybe that's because America and cars

ESCORT
VALVOLINE
Mobil 1
BFGoodrich
JEN-SEN
duraflame
DIABLO
CUSTOM ALIGNMENT
MASTER
Hella
71

GOODYEAR VR50 TIRES
The standard tire and wheel combination features P255/50VR 16 Goodyear unidirectional steel-belted radial tires mounted on 16" aluminum alloy wheels with functional turbine-blade design and anti-theft nuts.

ROOF PANEL STORAGE (COUPE)
The removable one-piece roof panel combines the security of a closed car with the exhilarating effects of an open roadster. There is no T-bar. The roof is removed using a ratchet wrench designed for this application. The panel may then be stored within the car in a lockdown position.

HALOGEN FOG LAMPS
The integral halogen fog lamps make driving under adverse conditions easier. Operation is independent of the headlamps.

CLOTH BUCKET SEATS
The high-back cloth bucket seats are contoured to provide the feeling of individualized fit and comfort. Manual back angle adjustment is offered. Other interior features include a leather-wrapped steering wheel, dual rear lockable storage compartments,* lighted visor vanity mirror.

TILT-TELESCOPIC STEERING WHEEL
Corvette adjusts to your driving style with a steering wheel that tilts and telescopes.

4-SPEED AUTOMATIC TRANSMISSION
Four-speed automatic overdrive transmission with lockup torque converter contributes to impressive performance plus low-RPM highway cruising.

4-SPEED MANUAL TRANSMISSION
If you prefer, choose the smooth-shifting manual 4-speed, with an electronic automatic overdrive feature in 2nd, 3rd and 4th gear, which is available at no extra cost. Gear ratios are chosen to deliver exceptional performance.

CORVETTE NEWS
A three-year complimentary subscription goes to every Corvette buyer. This publication keeps owners up to date on their favorite sports car.

*Coupe only.

CORVETTE'S AIR CONDITIONING ALLOWS YOU TO MAINTAIN A PERFECT DRIVING ENVIRONMENT.

RETRACTABLE HEADLAMPS FLIP FORWARD 162.5 DEGREES FROM BENEATH THE HOOD.

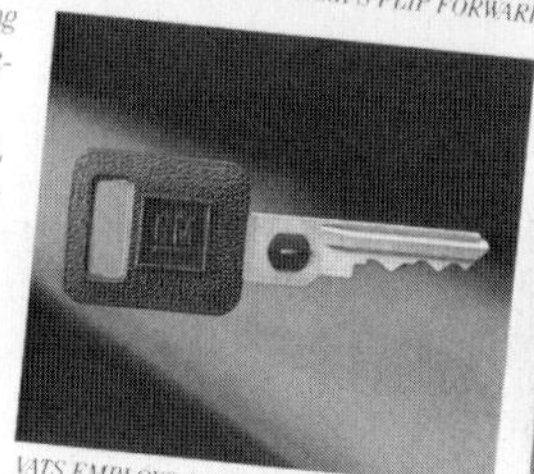

VATS EMPLOYS A DECODER AND IGNITION KEY WITH A PELLET OF SPECIFIED RESISTANCE.

GOODYEAR EAGLE GT P255/50VR 16 UNIDIRECTIONAL RADIAL TIRES.

THE REMOVABLE ONE-PIECE ROOF LIFT-OFF PANEL STORES IN A LOCKDOWN POSITION IN THE REAR COMPARTMENT, OPENING CORVETTE UP TO SUN AND STARS.

Motorsport: gewiß kein vorder gründiges Corvette-Thema – aber sehr fotogen . . .

Das Herz der '86er Corvette – der 5,74-Liter-V8-Motor mit gemäßigten 208 PS. Kraftstoff-Einspritzung ist mittlerweile zur Selbstverständlichkeit geworden.

CORVETTE, A GENERATION:
25 YEARS OF MEN, MACHINES, AND MEMORIES.

1953 – 1955
Januar 1953: Harley Earl präsentiert die Corvette auf der New Yorker Motorama-Show. Im Mai 1953 ist der Wagen reif für die Serienfertigung, vier Wochen später erscheint das erste Exemplar einer 300-Stück-Serie. Im September 1954 ist auch ein V8-Motor erhältlich. Der Roadster erhält im Herbst 1955 Kurbelscheiben und ein Hardtop.

1956 – 1957
Im September 1956 wird die Corvette mit Benzineinspritzung versehen. Für das Modelljahr 1958 bekommt der Wagen Doppelscheinwerfer und mehr Chrom.

Corvette – Auto einer Generation

1958 – 1960
GM-Designer Bill Mitchell arbeitet an einem Modell mit neuer Karosserie; es wird später als Sting Ray berühmt. Im Sommer 1960 wird die 10 000. Corvette des laufenden Modelljahrgangs hergestellt. Mit neuem Heck präsentiert man den 1961er Wagen.

1961 – 1962
Im Februar 1961 gibt der Sting Ray als Show Car in Chicago sein Debüt. Im Dezember 1962 testet man Scheibenbremsen und stärkere V8-Motoren.

1963 – 1967
Ab Ende 1963 weist das Heckfenster des Coupés keinen Steg mehr auf. Ein Jahr später bekommt die Corvette rungsum Scheibenbremsen. 6,5- und 7-Liter-Motoren werden angeboten. Das Modell 1966 wird stilistisch überarbeitet; die Motoren haben keine Einspritzung mehr. Im April 1967 kommt eine Hochleistungs-Version (L88) heraus mit 435 PS (und ohne Heizungsanlage).

1968 – 1977
Stark überarbeitetes Karosserie- und Interieur-Design, ähnlich dem Show Car „Mako Shark II". Im November 1969 verläßt die 250 000. Corvette das Werk in St. Louis. Im Februar 1970 stellt GM einen neuen 7,5-Liter-Motor – bis 460 PS stark – vor. Karosserieretuschen im Herbst 1973. Große Feierlichkeiten bei General Motors: Im März 1977 wird die 500 000. Corvette gebaut.

(aus einem Prospekt im Frühjahr 1978)

CORVETTE

Bücher für den Corvette-Liebhaber

Chevrolet – A History from 1911 – von Beverly Rae Kimes und Robert Ackerson. Die Corvette findet in diesem Geschichtsbuch ihren gebührenden Platz; vor allem sind die Farbfotos exzellent. Das Buch umfaßt insgesamt 200 Seiten mit 160 meist farbigen Fotos.

Corvette, an American Legend – vom Verlag Automobile Quarterly. Eines der ausführlichsten und bestgemachten Bücher zum Thema Corvette. Insbesondere werden Wagen der Baujahre 1953 bis 1967 eines bestimmten Wettbewerbs (Bloomington) behandelt, die absolut originalgetreu sind. 184 Seiten, 200 sehr gute Bilder in Farbe. Englischer Text.

Corvette – von B. Coleman. Eine Zusammenfassung der Corvette-Historie auf 100 Seiten (1953–1983) mit 100 Fotos, die meisten farbig. Ein guter Überblick (engl. Text) zur Schnell-Information.

Classic Corvettes in a Nutshell – von John F. Ball. Kaufberatung vom Fachmann, voller nützlicher Tips (engl. Sprache). 102 Seiten, 22 Abbildungen.

Corvette 1953–1967, A Source Book – von Arthur A.C. Steffen. Auf 144 Seiten Faksimile-Drucke von alten Werbemitteln und Inseraten, auch Händler-Informationen von General Motors. Eine interessante Quelle authentischer Unterlagen „aus der Zeit" mit über 300 Abbildungen.

Corvette – the Legend lives on. Die Fortsetzung des Bloomington-Themas für Wagen der Baujahre 1968 bis 1982, von Automobile Quarterly (siehe oben). 200 Seiten, 250 Farbfotos.

Early Chevrolet Corvettes – von C. Falconer. Ein Band der Auto-History-Serie (engl. Sprache). Alle Sechs- und Achtzylinder 1953–1967 werden hier beschrieben. 136 Seiten, 60 Schwarzweiß-Abbildungen, 8 Farbseiten.

Corvette Performance – alles über die Entwicklung dieses Wagens als Sport- und Rennfahrzeug (engl. Text). Renn- und Testberichte, Clubinformationen. 458 Abbildungen auf 180 Seiten.

Corvette, Amerikas Sportwagen – von Jay Koblenz. Ein in deutscher Sprache im Serag-Verlag erschienenes Buch von 256 Seiten Umfang der gesamten Geschichte des amerikanischen Zweisitzers. 250 Schwarzweiß- und 145 Farbaufnahmen. Ein lesenswertes und gut aufgemachtes Buch für den Enthusiasten.

The Complete Book of the Corvette – von Richard M. Langworth. Der prominente amerikanische Automobilhistoriker schrieb diesen hervorragend aufgemachten Band, der alle Modelle bis einschließlich 1987 vorstellt. 320 Seiten, über 400 vorwiegend farbige Abbildungen.

Corvette 1953–1980 Identification and Number Codes. Alle Chassisnummern und Motordaten, Getriebe-Spezifikationen und so fort für die Baujahre von 1953 bis 1980, auch Lackierungen (ab 1963) und Extras. Für den Besitzer einer Corvette – der es ganz genau wissen will – ein wertvolles Nachschlagewerk.

Corvette Restoration Handbook. Eine Restaurierungsanleitung für den Amateur, sehr gut abgefaßt, mit mehr als 300 Abbildungen (engl. Text) auf 248 Seiten. Alle Modelle bis 1967 finden Berücksichtigung.

Corvette Sting Ray – von Robert Ackerson. Ein Super-Profile-Band mit ausführlicher Typengeschichte, Restaurierungstips und Literatur-Verzeichnis. 56 Seiten, 20 farbige Abbildungen.

Corvette, Sports Car for America – von M.B. Antonick. Eine gut aufgemachte Rückblende auf die Entwicklungsgeschichte der Corvette von 1953 bis 1955, mit zeitgenössischen Werbemitteln und anderen Abbildungen. 240 Seiten, 200 Schwarzweiß- und 55 Farbfotos. Englischer Text. Der Autor hat auch ein weiteres Buch über die Corvette verfaßt, das nur spezielle Wettbewerbswagen behandelt.

The Complete Corvette Restoration & Technical Guide – von N. Adams. Ein teures, aber unentbehrliches Werk für den Restaurator. Mit 1400 Abbildungen auf 424 Seiten. Gründlicher und informativer geht's nicht! Englischer Text.

The Road Corvette – von R. Miller und G. Embree. Über 100 Fotos aller Modelle und Derivate von 1953 bis 1973 enthält dieses Buch, das zu den Klassikern der Corvette-Literatur gehört. Es hat 320 Seiten und enthält unter anderem sämtliche technischen Daten im Detail.

Corvette Body Repair Guide – von Robert J. Schiro. Für die Reparatur der Kunststoff-Karosserie ein wertvoller Helfer. Alle Vorgänge werden in Bildern gezeigt (250 Abbildungen, auch in Farbe). Das Buch ist spiralgebunden und umfaßt 200 Seiten.

(Es gibt noch etliche weitere Publikationen, sämtlich aus amerikanischen Verlagen, sowie Buyers Guides und Straßentest-Reprints. Die Automobilbuch-Versandhäuser und -Fachgeschäfte bieten eine umfassende Auswahl an einschlägiger Corvette-Literatur.)

Schrader-Motor-Chronik

Eine große Reihe mit Zukunft

Interessante Dokumentationen in Faksimile, zusammengestellt anhand zeitgenössischen Werbe- und Pressematerials in Schwarzweiß und Farbe. Jeder Band enthält eine Vielzahl von Abbildungen, technischen Angaben und Daten, basierend auf authentischen Werksveröffentlichungen.

Alfa Romeo Giulia u. Giulietta, Berlina, Sprint, Spider 1954-78 ISBN 3-922617-50-6 Best.-Nr. 22050	Alfa Romeo Spider 1955-86 ISBN 3-922617-13-1 Best.-Nr. 22013	Austin-Healey 100/4, 100/6, 3000, Sprite Mk. I-IV 1953-72 ISBN 3-922617-20-4 Best.-Nr. 22020	BMW Isetta und ihre Konkurrenten, 1955-62 ISBN 3-922617-10-7 Best.-Nr. 22010	BMW 501-507 Limousinen, Cabriolets, 3200 Bertone 1952-68 ISBN 3-922617-28-X Best.-Nr. 22028	BMW 1500-2002 1962-77 ISBN 3-922617-46-8 Best.-Nr. 22046	Chevrolet Corvette 1953-86 ISBN 3-922617-51-4 Best.-Nr. 22051
Citroën 2CV 1948-86 ISBN 3-922617-40-9 Best.-Nr. 22040	DKW-Auto Union Zweizyl., 3=6, AU 1000/S/SP 1950-65 ISBN 3-922617-60-3 Best.-Nr. 22060	Ferrari V12 365/400/412/512/ Testarossa 1972-86 ISBN 3-922617-35-2 Best.-Nr. 22035	Fiat 500/600 mit Topolino, Jagst, Multipla u. Weinsberg 1936-69 ISBN 3-922617-26-3 Best.-Nr. 22026	Fiat Sportwagen Coupés und Spider 1948-86 ISBN 3-922617-39-5 Best.-Nr. 22039	Ford Taunus 12M/15M, 1952-62 ISBN 3-922617-22-0 Best.-Nr. 22022	Goggomobil und Isar 600/700 1955-69 ISBN 3-922617-17-4 Best.-Nr. 22017
Jaguar E-Type 1961-75 ISBN 3-922617-42-5 Best.-Nr. 22042	Jeep 1942-86 ISBN 3-922617-29-8 Best.-Nr. 22029	Karmann Ghia Coupés und Cabriolets 1955-74 ISBN 3-922617-62-X Best.-Nr. 22062	Lancia Ardea, Aprilia, Aurelia, Appia, Flaminia, Flavia, Fulvia 46-72 ISBN 3-922617-97-2 Best.-Nr. 22097	Lanz Bulldog-Ackerschlepper, Straßenzugmaschinen 1928-55 ISBN 3-922617-56-5 Best.-Nr. 22056	Mercedes-Benz Cabriolets vom 170 u. 220 - 280 SE 3.5 V8 1949-71 ISBN 3-922617-77-8 Best.-Nr. 22077	Mercedes-Benz Heckflosse 220, 190/200, 230, 300 SE 1959-65 ISBN 3-922617-34-4 Best.-Nr. 22034
Mercedes-Benz Lastwagen u. Omnibusse 1947-61 ISBN 3-922617-38-7 Best.-Nr. 22038	Mercedes-Benz Ponton 180/D, 190/D, 219, 220, 220S/SE 1953-62 ISBN 3-922617-43-3 Best.-Nr. 22043	MGA-MGB-MGC Roadster und Coupés 1955-1981 ISBN 3-922617-67-0 Best.-Nr. 22067	Mini-Austin, Morris, Cooper S, Special, Clubman, 1275 GT 1959-83 ISBN 3-922617-55-7 Best.-Nr. 22055	Morgan Sport- und Tourenwagen 1935-81 ISBN 3-922617-78-6 Best.-Nr. 22078	NSU Ro 80 und Wankel Spider 1964-77 ISBN 3-922617-49-2 Best.-Nr. 22049	Porsche 356 1948-65 ISBN 3-922617-41-7 Best.-Nr. 22041
Porsche 911 mit Targa, Carrera, Cabriolet, 1963-86 ISBN 3-922617-27-1 Best.-Nr. 22027	Saab Automobile, Modelle 92 bis 99 u. Sonett, 1947-70 ISBN 3-921796-06-7 Best.-Nr. 22106	Triumph Spitfire + GT6 1962-80 ISBN 3-922617-95-6 Best.-Nr. 22095	Triumph TR2-TR8 1953-81 ISBN 3-922617-36-0 Best.-Nr. 22036	Volvo PV 444/544, Amazon 121, 122, 123 GT, P 1800 S/E/ES 1945-73 ISBN 3-922617-90-5 Best.-Nr. 22090	VW Käfer Cabrio, Karmann Ghia, Rometsch etc. 1949-80 ISBN 3-922617-15-8 Best.-Nr. 22015	VW Käfer Limousinen 1938-78 ISBN 3-922617-68-9 Best.-Nr. 22068
VW Transporter / Bus 1949-67 ISBN 3-922617-09-3 Best.-Nr. 22009	BMW Motorräder Einzyl. R24- R27, 1949-67 ISBN 3-922617-19-0 Best.-Nr. 22019	BMW Motorräder Zweizyl. R51/2-R75/5, 1950-73 ISBN 3-922617-54-9 Best.-Nr. 22054	Deutsche Motorroller v. Achilles, Dürkopp bis Vict. u. Zünd. 1949-73 ISBN 3-922617-94-8 Best.-Nr. 22094	Dtsch. Seitenwg.-Motorr. von Adler u. BMW, Triumph u. Zündapp ISBN 3-922617-52-2 Best.-Nr. 22052	DKW Motorräder Vorkriegsmodelle, 1922-39 ISBN 3-921796-07-5 Best.-Nr. 22107	DKW Motorräder 1949-58 ISBN 3-922617-47-6 Best.-Nr. 22047
Harley-Davidson Singles u. Twins, Motorräder 1918-78 ISBN 3-922617-61-1 Best.-Nr. 22061	Horex Regina bis Imperator 1950-56 ISBN 3-922617-12-3 Best.-Nr. 22012	Moto Guzzi Motorräder 1946-76 ISBN 3-922617-98-0 Best.-Nr. 22098	NSU Motorräder 1949-63 ISBN 3-922617-32-8 Best.-Nr. 22032	Triumph Motorräder 1903 - 57 ISBN 3-922617-89-1 Best.-Nr. 22089	Vespa-Motorroller mit Vespa 400 u. Piaggio Dreirad 1948-86 ISBN 3-922617-25-5 Best.-Nr. 22025	Zündapp Motorräder 1947-84 ISBN 3-922617-37-9 Best.-Nr. 22037

Schrader (S) Verlag

Die Corvette in der Presse

Im August 1953 erschienen in der amerikanischen Motorpresse die ersten Berichte über die neue Corvette. Sie gingen über eine Modellbeschreibung kaum hinaus – Straßentests wurden nicht vor dem Frühjahr 1954 veröffentlicht. In **Road & Track** las sich ein erster Eindruck so:

,,Schon seit 1948 erhoben wir immer wieder die Frage nach einem amerikanischen Sportwagen. Jetzt haben wir ihn in Gestalt der Chevrolet Corvette. Allerdings stellten wir anläßlich einer Testfahrt nach Chicago und New York fest, daß dieses Auto bei Sportwagen-Enthusiasten noch kaum bekannt ist – und manche glauben auch gar nicht, daß dieses Auto auch wirklich ein Sportwagen ist!'' So gab sich John R. Bond Mühe, seine Leser davon zu überzeugen. Er zitierte die von Maurice Olley niedergelegten Konstruktions-Vorgaben und nannte die Corvette einen ,,angenehmen Kontrast zu vielen Pseudo-Sportwagen, wie sie unter anderen General-Motors-Marken angeboten werden''. Dennoch: Zwischen den Zeilen standen ein paar Fragezeichen.

Als die Corvette mit V8-Motor erschien, gab sich die Motorpresse schon fröhlicher. Doch es blieb Kritik am Getriebe und an den Bremsen: ,,Davon ist der Enthusiast nicht zu überzeugen. Was soll auch der Slogan – For Experts only –? Es gehört keine besondere Begabung dazu, die Corvette zu fahren . . .'' Was man sich wünschte, war vor allem ein Getriebe mit Handschaltung. Und die hatte man endlich im 1956er Modell zu testen Gelegenheit. **Road & Track** schrieb: ,,Auf den ersten Blick meint man, drei Gänge sind nicht ausreichend. Doch die Übersetzungen sind ausgezeichnet abgestuft. 100 Meilen in zweiten Gang! Diese neue Corvette verspricht ein sehr interessanter Wagen für den Liebhaber zu werden, der ein gutes Allroundfahrzeug sucht. Es dürfte sogar Chancen in der Serienwagenklasse C (3 bis 5 Liter) haben und dort für eine gewisse Belebung sorgen . . .''

Als ,,gut bis ausgezeichnet'' beurteilten Journalisten von **Sports Car Illustrated** die 1956er Corvette. Sie stellten vor allem die Beschleunigung heraus, gemessen mit 7,4 Sekunden vom Stand auf 100 km/h. Als Spitzentempo wurden 130 Meilen = 209 km/h gemessen. Allerdings stellte man auch einige Vibrationen bei hohem Tempo fest, was auch **Road & Track** konstatierte: ,,Schütteler-scheinungen bei mehr als 100 Meilen gab es früher nicht, auch ist die Maschine, wie es scheint, etwas laut geworden . . .''

Die 1958er Corvette wurde wieder mit viel Euphorie begrüßt. ,,Zwei Vierfachvergaser oder Benzineinspritzung bei einer Kompression von 10,5 : 1! Ein Drehzahlmesser

Nr. 867 Chevrolet Corvette Sport-Cabriolet

Ausrüstung	Türen: 2	
	Synchromesh-Getriebe	
	Scheibenwaschanlage	
	Heizung und Entfroster	
	Handbrems-Warnlicht	
	Uhr	
	Elektrisch betätigtes Verdeck	
	Abnehmbares Kunststoff-Hardtop	
Motor	Steuer-PS	23,62
	Brems-PS bei U/Min.	233/4800
	Anzahl Zylinder	8
	Zylinderinhalt cm³	4637
	Bohrung mm	98,42
	Hub mm	76,20
	Kompressionsverhältnis	9,5:1
	Verhältnis Brems-PS zu Gewicht kg/PS	6,1
Getriebe	Synchromesh-Getriebeuntersetzung	I: 2,2:1
		II: 1,66:1
		III: 1,31:1
		IV: 1:1
		R: 2,26:1
	Hinterachse	3,7:1
Abmessungen und Gewichte	Länge mm	4488
	Breite mm	1788
	Höhe mm	1320
	Leergewicht fahrbereit kg	1430
	Radstand mm	2591
	Spur vorn mm	1448
	Spur hinten mm	1499
	Spurkreisdurchmesser m	11,10
	Pneugrösse	7,3×15
	Benzintankinhalt l	62

bis 8000 Touren! Eine kräftiger dimensionierte Kupplung und ein selbsthemmendes Differential! Dreiganggetriebe oder Viergangautomatik zur Wahl! Sportfahrer wie auch Komfort-Liebhaber kommen voll auf ihre Kosten . . ."
Die häufigen stilistischen Änderungen, in den USA gang und gäbe, stießen nie auf Kritik. Das Cockpit, so befand die Presse, gerate von Jahr zu Jahr besser, nur sei es (1959) an der Zeit, der Corvette Sicherheitsgurte zu geben „für hartes Fahren" – obligatorisch waren sie noch nicht. Ansonsten gab es nur zwei Punkte zu kritisieren: eine gewisse Übersteuerungstendenz und ein zu langsames Ansprechen des Motors beim Druck aufs Gaspedal, was bei Schaltvorgängen zu unerwünschten Beschleunigungspausen führte.
Hin und wieder wurde auch die Kunststoff-Karosserie kritisch erwähnt, doch man konnte ihr keine Mängel nachsagen. „Sie ist tadellos verarbeitet, die Übergänge einzelner Teile sind perfekt. Man merkt, daß sich Chevrolet bei der Karosserie sehr viel Mühe gibt." Großes Lob bekamen die Sitze: „Sehr gut ausgeformt und komfortabel. Auch bei längeren Reisen keine Ermüdung am Steuer. Ein Tag in der Corvette ist kein Streß!" (1961).
Als der Sting Ray seine Aufwartung machte, wurde er mit Applaus begrüßt. Sogar die **New York Times** widmete ihm ausführlich Raum: „Wirklich gelungen! Innerhalb von zehn Jahren hat sich Amerikas einziger Sport-

Einer der wenigen Prospekte in deutscher Sprache (für die Schweiz) beschränkte sich auf die Angabe technischer Daten und die Aufzählung der General-Motors-Händler.

Chevrolet-Vertretungen in der Schweiz
Distributeurs Chevrolet en Suisse

Aadorf	Eugen Ruckstuhl, Garage, Tel. (052) 4 73 19
Aarau	F. Glaus & Co., Hohlgass-Garage, Tel. (064) 2 13 33
Baden	B. Leoni AG, Bruggerstrasse 50, Tel. (056) 2 38 38
Basel	Agence Américaine Automobiles S.A., Viaduktstr. 45 (Postfach 105), Tel. (061) 24 66 66
Bern	Bellevue-Garage AG, Kochergasse 1, Tel. (031) 3 77 77
Bern	Gebr. Bärtschi AG, Länggass-Garage, Tel. (031) 3 36 33
Bern	Spiegl & Waber GmbH, Nordring 8, Tel. (031) 9 44 44
Bern	Hans Lack, Ostring-Garage, Freudenbergerplatz Tel. (031) 4 49 11
Biel	Burkhalter & Brändli, Garage, Freiestrasse 7, Tel. (032) 2 25 24
Buchs/SG	A. Sulser, Garage, Tel. (085) 6 14 14
La Chaux-de-Fonds	Garage Guttmann S.A., 110, rue de la Serre, tél. (039) 3 46 81
Chur	L. Dosch, Grand-Garage, Tel. (081) 2 13 13
Fribourg	L. & M. Baudère, Garage de Pérolles, tél. (037) 2 38 88
Genève	Etabl. Fleury & Cie S.A., rue de la Mairie 35, tél. (022) 36 62 30
Glarus	F. Schielly-Ryffel, Central-Garage, Tel. (058) 5 18 34
Interlaken	E. Zimmermann, Bahnhof-Garage, Tel. (036) 2 13 15
Langenthal	M. & E. Würgler, Garage, Tel. (063) 2 20 77
Lausanne	Etabl. Ch. Ramuz S.A., avenue d'Echallens 2a, tél. (021) 24 04 44
Liestal	Blank AG, Tiergartenweg 1, Tel. (061) 84 31 11
Lugano	Eredi di N. Crescionini, Via Stefano Franscini 8, tel. (091) 2 83 43
Luzern	Auto-Koch AG, Löwenplatz, Tel. (041) 2 77 77
Münsingen	Ernst Marti, Garage, Tel. (031) 68 15 15
Neuchâtel	Garage Schenker, Faubourg du Lac 29, tél. (038) 5 28 64
Porrentruy	Périat & Pétignat, Garage des Ponts, tél (066) 6 12 06
Reiden	Turmgarage, Luzernerstrasse, Tel. (062) 9 35 44
Sarnen	Cl. Sidler, Garage, Brünigstrasse, Tel. (041) 85 18 88
Schaffhausen/Neuhausen	Georg Neck, Garage Enge, Tel. (053) 6 94 55
Schattdorf	A. Brand-Stadler, Autogarage, Tel. (044) 2 13 88
Sion	G. Revaz, Garage de l'Ouest, tél. (027) 2 22 62
Solothurn	E. Kupferschmid & O. Müller, Tel. (065) 2 14 42
St. Gallen	E. Wagner, Centralgarage AG, Tel. (071) 22 55 22
St. Maurice	Jean-Jacques Casanova, Garage, tél. (025) 3 63 90
St. Moritz	Gebr. Cattaneo, Kulm-Garage, Tel. (082) 3 33 33
Sursee	O. & R. Wyder, Automobile, Bahnhofstrasse, Tel. (045) 4 22 22
Thun	Paul Wenger, Oberland-Garage, Tel. (033) 2 30 29
Weinfelden	J. Ammann-Grünert, Central-Garage, Tel. (072) 5 13 33
Wetzikon	B. Krähenmann, Werkgarage, Usterstrasse 46, Tel. (051) 97 87 02
Wil	Fürstenland-Garage AG, Tel. (073) 6 04 80
Winterthur	Eulach-Garage AG, Technikumstrasse 67, Tel. (052) 2 23 33
Yverdon	W. Humberset, Garage des Remparts, tél. (024) 2 35 35
Zug	Jos. Iten, Autos, Tel. (042) 4 23 23
Zürich	AG Vertretung Agence Américaine, Dufourstrasse 23, Tel. (051) 32 72 73

wagen zu einem reinrassigen Fahrzeug gemausert, für Straßen und Sport gleichermaßen ausgezeichnet geeignet.''

Die ausgewogene Gewichtsverteilung und die Einzelradaufhängung wurden besonders herausgestellt. **Motor Trend** schrieb: ,,Ein bemerkenswerter Unterschied. Der Abstand zu europäischen Sportwagen ist aufgeholt!'' **Road & Track:** ,,Der neue Sting Ray klebt auf der Straße . . . vorbei ist die Zeit, als die Corvette mit den Hinterrädern Tänze aufführte wie ein Apache mit heißen Füßen!''

Bald war die Corvette mit Motoren bis zu 375 PS zu haben. ,,Obwohl so stark motorisiert, ist der Wagen lammfromm zu führen'', hieß es in einem **Road & Track**-Test 1964. Und in Verbindung mit der Viergang-Automatik sei so viel Power exzellent zu beherrschen. Der Zuspruch, dessen sich die Corvette nach zehn Jahren ihrer Existenz zu erfreuen habe, sei enorm gewachsen und mit Porsche vergleichbar. Und: ,,Endlich hat man die Teilung der Heckscheibe wegfallen lassen – eine wesentliche Verbesserung der Sicht nach hinten.'' Man beeilte sich auch hinzuzufügen, daß die Schlafaugen-Scheinwerfer kein Gag der Stylisten in Detroit seien, sondern aerodynamische Vorteile brächten.

,,Es gibt im Sting Ray auch Platz fürs Gepäck – nur muß es über die Sitze verstaut werden, denn der Wagen hat keine Kofferklappe. Gut wäre es, man könnte die Heckscheibe wie beim Aston Martin öffnen'' (ein Wunsch, der später bei einem Sondermodell in Erfüllung ging). ,,Kritik möchten wir auch an den Platzverhältnissen üben: Der Fahrer sitzt recht beengt – im Vergleich zu den großzügigen Gesamtabmessungen des Wagens.'' Ansonsten: Höchste Anerkennung über den qualitativen Verarbeitungsstandard.

Im August 1965 wurde ein 425-PS-Wagen der Presse zur Verfügung gestellt. ,,Man würde sich wünschen, daß diese Corvette im Rennsport Furore macht . . . aber leider dürfte der Wagen dafür zu viel Gewicht haben'', schrieb **Road & Track.** In der Tat: Die Corvette war 400 Kilogramm schwerer als die Cobra. ,,Es kommt bekanntlich nicht auf die Zahl der Pferdestärken an, sondern wieviele man davon zum Nutzen auf den Boden bringt . . . Viele Sportwagen hätten mehr Pfeffer nötig gehabt, aber die Corvette gehörte eigentlich nicht zu ihnen.'' In den siebziger Jahren wußte die Presse nicht viel Neues über ,,Amerikas einzigen Sportwagen'' zu berichten. Man wiederholte die Hoffnungen und Erwartungen hinsichtlich motorsportlicher Engagements, auch in der europäischen Motorpresse.

Eines kurzen Schlaglichts erfreute sich die berühmte Renn-Corvette, die 1957 von Zora Arkus-Duntov präpariert worden war, in der deutschen Motorpresse. **Auto, motor und sport** berichtete über dieses Fahrzeug (,,das einzige Auto, mit dem sich General Motors jemals offiziell am Rennsport beteiligte'') und schrieb:

,,Weil die Zeit drängte, entkleidete Duntov ein Mercedes 300 SL Coupé und kopierte den Rohrrahmen. Gerüchte zu jener Zeit besagten zwar, daß der Rahmen dem des Jaguar D-Type nachgebaut wurde, doch beweist ein damals gemachtes Foto, daß es sich doch um einen 300-SL-Rahmen handelte. Er bestand aus dreieckförmig angeordneten Rohren aus Chrom-Molybdänstahl. Vorn und hinten waren stärkere Rohre zur Aufnahme der Radaufhängungen montiert.''

Die Karosserien – es gab eine aus Leichtmetall und eine aus Kunststoff – wogen je 82 Kilogramm – genausoviel wie der Rohrrahmen. ,,Die Corvette SS geriet sehr viel leichter und kleiner als die Serienausführung . . . das Gesamtgewicht betrug nur 900 Kilogramm.''

Die ersten Probefahrten, so wird berichtet, seien von Fangio und Moss absolviert worden. Im Sebring-Rennen fuhren den Wagen John Fitch und Piero Taruffi. Doch die Corvette SS beendete das Rennen nicht – wegen einer ganzen Reihe kleinerer, aber letztlich ent-

Berichterstattung über die 250 Meilen von Daytona in „sportauto", Januar 1976. Die Corvette des Amerikaners John Greenwood hatte 725 PS unter der Haube.

scheidender Pannen. Der Wagen kam später ins Museum – er wurde nie mehr eingesetzt.
Privat eingesetzte Exemplare tauchten indessen an zahlreichen Rundstreckenrennen immer wieder auf, in den USA und auch anderswo – mit unterschiedlichem Erfolg. Ein hochfrisierter Sting Ray mit über 700 PS beteiligte sich zum Beispiel an den 250 Meilen von Daytona 1976 und anderen Wettbewerben. Yörn Pugmeister berichtete in **sport auto** über das Corvette-Monster:
,,Die äußere Form erinnert noch an ‚den' amerikanischen Sportwagen, aber John Greenwood schuf sich seine eigene Corvette. Dazu fräste er erst einmal das Chassis des Ursprungsautos weitgehend weg und ersetzte es durch einen Rohrrahmen; dann spendierte er dem Mobil neue Bremsen vorn und hinten . . .'' Als Motor installierte Greenwood einen 8,2 Liter mit 725 PS. Mit einem Schnitt von 188 km/h wurde Greenwood als Sieger abgewunken – mehr als eine halbe Minute vor Brian Redman auf einem BMW 3,0 CSL.
Die Corvette der frühen achtziger Jahre gab ebenfalls – noch – zu keinen Klagen Anlaß. ,,Power ist genügend vorhanden; in 7,2 Sekunden ist man auf 100 km/h'', schrieb John Lamm 1983. ,,Aber die Corvette bietet mehr als nur Tempo. Zum Beispiel einen völlig neuen Sitzkomfort. Jezt hat man nicht mehr das Gefühl, in einem riesigen Schuh zu sitzen, der dennoch zu eng ist . . .'' Es gebe eine gute Rundumsicht, eine überaus reichhaltige Instrumentierung (wahlweise auf metrische Anzeige umschaltbar, was sehr begrüßt wurde) und erfreulicherweise keine überflüssigen Mätzchen. ,,Ist die Corvette der beste Exote der Welt?'' Man verglich sie mit einem Porsche 928 S und einem Ferrari 308 GTBi und kam zu dem Schluß, daß der Amerikaner gar nicht so schlecht abschneide . . . Vor allem sei der Wagen im Design seinen europäischen Rivalen überlegen (meinte Autor Jonathan Thompson): ,,Er ist das am besten aussehende Auto, das heute auf dem Markt ist . . . sowohl aufregend als auch geschmackvoll und elegant . . . Mit dieser Corvette haben sich die Schlaglichter der Karosserie-Designbranche von Europa nach Amerika herübergewendet . . .'' Ein Kompliment, das Jerry Palmer zugedacht war, dem ,,Corvette Body Designer'', der auch für den Camaro und Chevrolet Vega verantwortlich gezeichnet hatte.

Dreamcar der neunziger Jahre: Der 1989 in Genf gezeigte Chevrolet Corvette mit 5,7-Liter-Motor, ein Vierventiler mit allen Attributen modernen Hochleistungs-Motorenbaus.

Modell-jahr	Motoren-spezifikation		Gemischaufbereitung	Anmerkungen
1953	6 Zylinder Blue Flame		3 Flachstrom-Vergaser	300 Vorserienwagen; alle weiß
1954	235 c.i. (3858 ccm)	150 PS/4200 ohv	3 Flachstrom-Vergaser	Farbe jetzt auch rot; blau; kupfer
1955	Blue Flame 235 c.i. (3858 ccm) Turbo Fire V-8 265 c.i. (4343 ccm)	155 PS/4200 ohv 195 PS/4400	3 Flachstrom-Vergaser 1 Fallstrom-Vierfach-Vergaser	Neu: V8-Motor; 12-Volt-Anlage; Einige Wagen mit 3-Gang-Schaltung
1956	V-8 265 c.i. (4343 ccm)	210 PS/5200 ohv 225 PS/5200 ohv	1 Fallstrom-Vierfach-Vergaser 2 Fallstrom-Vierfach-Vergaser	Neue Karosserie; 3-Gang-Getriebe; Auf Wunsch Powerglide
1957	V-8 283 c.i. (4638 ccm) Competition	220 PS/4800 ohv 245 PS/5000 ohv 250 PS/5000 ohv 283 PS/6200 ohv	1 Fallstrom-Vierfach-Vergaser 2 Fallstrom-Vierfach-Vergaser Ramjet Fuel Injection Ramjet Fuel Injection	Auf Wunsch Viergang-Schaltung
1958	V-8 283 c.i. (4638 ccm) Competition	230 PS/4800 ohv 245 PS/5000 ohv 250 PS/5000 ohv 290 PS/6200 ohv	1 Fallstrom-Vierfach-Vergaser 2 Fallstrom-Vierfach-Vergaser Ramjet Fuel Injection Ramjet Fuel Injection	Neuer Grill und Doppelschein-werfer, mehr Chromschmuck
1959	V-8 283 c.i. (4638 ccm)	230 PS/4800 ohv 245 PS/5000 ohv 250 PS/5000 ohv 270 PS/5400 ohv 290 PS/6200 ohv	1 Fallstrom-Vierfach-Vergaser 2 Fallstrom-Vierfach-Vergaser Ramjet Fuel Injection 2 Fallstrom-Vierfach-Vergaser Ramjet Fuel Injection	Chrom wird wieder reduziert
1960	V-8 283 c.i. (4638 ccm)	230 PS/4800 ohv 245 PS/5000 ohv 270 PS/5400 ohv 275 PS/5800 ohv 315 PS/6400 ohv	1 Fallstrom-Vierfach-Vergaser 2 Fallstrom-Vierfach-Vergaser 2 Fallstrom-Vierfach-Vergaser Ramjet Fuel Injection Ramjet Fuel Injection	Auf Wunsch elektrische Fensterheber
1961	V-8 283 c.i. (4638 ccm)	wie 1960	wie 1960	Neuer Grill; neues Heck
1962	V-8 327 c.i. (5359 ccm)	250 PS/4400 ohv 300 PS/5000 ohv 340 PS/6000 ohv 360 PS/6000	1 Fallstrom-Vierfach-Vergaser 1 Fallstrom-Vierfach-Vergaser 1 Fallstrom-Vierfach-Vergaser Ramjet Fuel Injection	Neuer Motor „327“

Technische Daten

Modell- jahr	Motoren- spezifikation		Gemischaufbereitung	Anmerkungen
1963	V-8 327 c.i. (5359 ccm)	wie 1962	wie 1962	Neue Karosserie; Neu: Fastback-Coupé
1964	V-8 327 c.i. (5359 ccm)	250 PS/4400 ohv 300 PS/5000 ohv 365 PS/6200 ohv 375 PS/6200 ohv	1 Fallstrom-Vierfach-Vergaser 1 Fallstrom-Vierfach-Vergaser 1 Fallstrom-Vierfach-Vergaser Fuel-Injection	Verstellbare Stoßdämpfer
1965	V-8 327 c.i. (5359 ccm) V-8 396 c.i. (6489 ccm)	250 PS/4400 ohv 300 PS/5000 ohv 350 PS/5800 ohv 365 PS/6200 ohv 375 PS/6200 ohv PS/4800 ohv	1 Fallstrom-Vierfach-Vergaser 1 Fallstrom-Vierfach-Vergaser 1 Fallstrom-Vierfach-Vergaser 1 Fallstrom-Vierfach-Vergaser Fuel-Injection 2 Fallstrom-Vierfach-Vergaser	Vier Scheibenbremsen
1966	V-8 327 c.i. (5359 ccm) Turbo-Jet 427 c.i. (6997 ccm) V-8	300 PS/5000 ohv 350 PS/5800 ohv 390 PS/5200 ohv 425 PS/5600 ohv	1 Fallstrom-Vierfach-Vergaser 1 Fallstrom-Vierfach-Vergaser 1 Fallstrom-Vierfach-Vergaser 1 Fallstrom-Vierfach-Vergaser	Neuer Turbo-Jet 427-c.i.-Motor
1967	V-8 327 c.i. (5359 ccm) Turbo-Jet 427 c.i. (6997 ccm) V-8	300 PS/5000 ohv 350 PS/5800 ohv 390 PS/5400 ohv 400 PS/5400 ohv 435 PS/5800 ohv	1 Fallstrom-Vierfach-Vergaser 1 Fallstrom-Vierfach-Vergaser 1 Fallstrom-Vierfach-Vergaser 3 Doppelvergaser 3 Doppelvergaser	Neue Doppelvergaser-Hochleistungsmotoren
1968	V-8 327 c.i. (5359 ccm) V-8 396 c.i. (6489 ccm) V-8 427 c.i. (6997 ccm)	300 PS/5000 ohv 350 PS/5200 ohv 390 PS/5400 ohv 400 PS/5400 ohv 435 PS/5800 ohv	1 Fallstrom-Vierfach-Vergaser 1 Fallstrom-Vierfach-Vergaser 1 Fallstrom-Vierfach-Vergaser 3 Doppelvergaser 3 Doppelvergaser	Neues Karosserie-Styling
1969	V-8 350 c.i. (5735 ccm) V-8 427 c.i. (6997 ccm)	300 PS/4800 ohv 350 PS/5600 ohv 390 PS/5400 ohv 400 PS/5400 ohv 425 PS/5600 ohv 430 PS/5200 ohv 435 PS/5800 ohv	1 Fallstrom-Vierfach-Vergaser 1 Fallstrom-Vierfach-Vergaser 1 Fallstrom-Vierfach-Vergaser 1 Fallstrom-Vierfach-Vergaser 1 Fallstrom-Vierfach-Vergaser 1 Fallstrom-Vierfach-Vergaser 3 Doppelvergaser	Neuer 350-c.i.-Motor

Technische Daten

Modelljahr	Motorenspezifikation		Gemischaufbereitung	Anmerkungen
1970	V-8 350 c.i. (5735 ccm)	300 PS/4800 ohv	1 Fallstrom-Vierfach-Vergaser	Neuer 454-c.i.-Motor
		350 PS/5600 ohv	1 Fallstrom-Vierfach-Vergaser	
		370 PS/6000 ohv	1 Fallstrom-Vierfach-Vergaser	
	V-8 454 c.i. (7440 ccm)	390 PS/4800 ohv	1 Fallstrom-Vierfach-Vergaser	
		460 PS/5600 ohv	1 Fallstrom-Vierfach-Vergaser	
1971	V-8 350 c.i. (5735 ccm)	270 PS/4800 ohv	1 Fallstrom-Vierfach-Vergaser	
		330 PS/5600 ohv	1 Fallstrom-Vierfach-Vergaser	
	V-8 454 c.i. (7440 ccm)	365 PS/4800 ohv	1 Fallstrom-Vierfach-Vergaser	
		425 PS/5600 ohv	1 Fallstrom-Vierfach-Vergaser	
1972	V-8 350 c.i. (5735 ccm)	200 PS/4400 ohv	1 Fallstrom-Vierfach-Vergaser	Drastische Leistungsminderungen durch neue Abgasgesetze
		255 PS/5600 ohv	1 Fallstrom-Vierfach-Vergaser	
	V-8 454 c.i. (7440 ccm)	270 PS/4000 ohv	1 Fallstrom-Vierfach-Vergaser	
1973	V-8 350 c.i. (5735 ccm)	190 PS/4400 ohv	1 Fallstrom-Vierfach-Vergaser	
		250 PS/5200 ohv	1 Fallstrom-Vierfach-Vergaser	
	V-8 454 c.i. (7440 ccm)	275 PS/4000 ohv	1 Fallstrom-Vierfach-Vergaser	
1974	V-8 350 c.i. (5735 ccm)	195 PS/4400 ohv	1 Fallstrom-Vierfach-Vergaser	Neues aufprallsicheres Heck
		250 PS/5200 ohv	1 Fallstrom-Vierfach-Vergaser	
	V-8 454 c.i. (7440 ccm)	270 PS/4400 ohv	1 Fallstrom-Vierfach-Vergaser	
1975	V-8 350 c.i. (5735 ccm)	198 PS/4400 ohv	1 Fallstrom-Vierfach-Vergaser	
		253 PS/5200 ohv	1 Fallstrom-Vierfach-Vergaser	
	V-8 454 c.i. (7440 ccm)	247 PS/4400 ohv	1 Fallstrom-Vierfach-Vergaser	
1976	V-8 350 c.i. (5735 ccm)	167 PS/3800 ohv	1 Fallstrom-Vierfach-Vergaser	
		208 PS/4800 ohv	1 Fallstrom-Vierfach-Vergaser	
1977	V-8 350 c.i. (5735 ccm)	183 PS/4000 ohv	1 Fallstrom-Vierfach-Vergaser	
		213 PS/5200 ohv	1 Fallstrom-Vierfach-Vergaser	
1978	V-8 350 c.i. (5735 ccm)	180 PS/4000 ohv	1 Fallstrom-Vierfach-Vergaser	Scheibenbremsen serienmäßig
		210 PS/5200 ohv	1 Fallstrom-Vierfach-Vergaser	
1979	V-8 350 c.i. (5735 ccm)	185 PS/4000 ohv	1 Fallstrom-Vierfach-Vergaser	Einzelradaufhängung hinten
		220 PS/5200 ohv	1 Fallstrom-Vierfach-Vergaser	

Technische Daten

Modelljahr	Motorenspezifikation		Gemischaufbereitung	Anmerkungen
1980	V-8 350 c.i. (5735 ccm)	195 PS/4000 ohv 225 PS/5200 ohv	1 Fallstrom-Vierfach-Vergaser 1 Fallstrom-Vierfach-Vergaser	Gewichtsreduzierung um 140 kg
1981	V-8 305 c.i. (5001 ccm) V-8 350 c.i. (5735 ccm)	186 PS/4200 ohv 197 PS/4400 ohv 238 PS/5200 ohv	1 Fallstrom-Vierfach-Vergaser 1 Fallstrom-Vierfach-Vergaser 1 Fallstrom-Vierfach-Vergaser	
1982	V-8 350 c.i. (5735 ccm)	197 PS/4400 ohv	1 Fallstrom-Vierfach-Vergaser	Collector edition: Aufklappbare Heckscheibe
1983	V-8 350 c.i. (5735 ccm)	204 PS/4200 ohv	Fuel Injection	Völlig neues Modell
1984/85	V-8 350 c.i. (5735 ccm)	208 PS/4200 ohv	Fuel Injection	
1986	V-8 350 c.i. (5735 ccm)	208 PS/4200 ohv	Fuel Injection	Neues Cabriolet

Technische Daten